Lazy Cook in the Kitchen

Mouthwatering recipes for the time-pressured cook

created by

Lazy Cook Mo Smith

Autumn to Easter

Lazy Cook in the Kitchen

Published in October 2000
by
BriCor
Cadogan Grange, Bisley,
Stroud, Glos. GL6 7AT

ISBN No 1 902100-23-9

website: www.lazycookmosmith.co.uk
Email: info@lazycookmosmith.co.uk

Written, compiled and edited by Mo Smith

Cover Design by Terry Cripps, SMC Bristol
Printed by: Leckhampton Printing Co., Cheltenham, Glos.

With grateful thanks to my family and the many

friends who have helped and encouraged me.

Contents

How I became a Lazy Cook

From as far back as I can remember I have been fascinated by cooking. At school it was the only lesson I enjoyed and one in which I succeeded where the remainder of the class struggled. This new-found skill filled me with enthusiasm and ambition – the ambition to be a cookery demonstrator. However, on leaving school at fifteen I was sent to a secretarial college and it was many years before this childhood ambition came to life. It happened shortly after we moved to the Cotswolds.

Our youngest child had started school when one day I read a piece in a national newspaper about a lady who was offering cookery demonstrations in her kitchen. I was reminded of my early desire to demonstrate cooking and with the children at school there was no reason for me to delay. I soon set about planning and it was not long before I was filling my kitchen with ladies eager to learn about my kind of cooking.

The success of these demonstrations created other opportunities for me and writing, broadcasting and public speaking were soon added to my curriculum. Over the years I have also followed many other interests all of which have kept me out of the kitchen. However, recipe development has continued to play an important part in my life and providing tasty meals, attractively presented is the only way I know how to cook - but with time against me I had to have a re-think.

I began by taking a new look at the present day ingredients available to me both in my store cupboard and on the supermarket shelves. Putting all my experience to the test, taking short cuts and speeding up on preparation and assembly, I built up a completely new collection of recipes - still tasty to eat and good to look at but very quick to prepare .... and so I became a "Lazy Cook".

Ever since I began creating my own recipes I have rarely ceased to be amazed by the number of different ways a handful of everyday ingredients can be prepared and presented offering a variety of colours, textures and flavours. As a new project I put a small collection of recipes in my first book – "Enter the new Millennium with Lazy Cook Mo Smith". The success of this publication and the enthusiastic feedback I received has encouraged me to offer more Lazy Cook recipes in this my second book.

Here you will discover over 150 mouthwatering recipes created for anyone who, like myself, enjoys eating well, but is pressured for time – enjoy!

MoSmith

I am currently broadcasting regularly with BBC Radio Gloucestershire.

Also available - "Enter the New Millennium with Lazy Cook Mo Smith" (1st published October 1999 – 1st reprint October 2000), over 90 Lazy Cook recipes, tips and anecdotes bound in a red cover. A perfect stocking filler or small present. Send £3.50 per copy (incl. postage & packing) to:-

Lazy Cook Mo Smith
Bear House
Bisley, Glos. GL6 7BB

website: www.lazycookmosmith.co.uk
Email: info@lazycookmosmith.co.uk

a percentage from each sale will be given to charity

Introduction to Recipes

The recipes in this book are divided into three sections - "Into Autumn", "The 12 days of Christmas" and "January to Easter" - although they can of course be switched about to suit your day to day catering throughout the year. Whatever the occasion, my Lazy Cook recipes will leave you with time and energy to enjoy it.

Into Autumn

As the evenings draw in, the trees display a final brilliance as the leaves turn from red to brown before falling. The season gradually changes and my thoughts turn from salads and barbecues in the garden to jacket potatoes, buttered pikelets, bowls of soup with hot bread and the many other foods which comfort us during the long autumn and winter months.

Index of Recipes

page

Main Courses

Puddings

Starters and Light Meals

Bacon and Potato Soup

serves 4
1 large onion – skin and chop
1 pkt (200gms) bacon lardons
900gms (2lbs) potatoes – peel and cut into small pieces
1 small turnip – peel and slice
1 ltr (2pts) stock
2 teas. Dijon mustard
several good pinches mixed dried herbs
nutmeg – freshly grated

Smear the base of a large pan with oil, add the onion and bacon lardons, stir well together, put lid on pan and cook for a few minutes before adding the remaining ingredients. Stir, bring to a simmer, skim the top then simmer with lid on pan for 30mins. or until the potatoes have softened. Taste and adjust the seasoning if necessary before serving.

Lazy Cook tips – if bacon lardons (ready chopped bacon) are not available cut up thinly sliced rindless streaky bacon. If a smoother soup is desired, puree all the solid ingredients together after cooking removing them with a slotted spoon into a food processor or liquidiser. A good winter soup. If you cook by Aga the simmering process should be done in the simmering oven.

Herring Roes with a Black Butter Sauce served on a bed of Salad Leaves

serves 4
225gms (8ozs) herring roes
a little flour seasoned with freshly ground pepper
50gms (2ozs) butter
a splash of balsamic vinegar
mixed salad leaves
freshly chopped parsley

Wash the roes and dry on kitchen roll. Melt half the butter in a shallow pan, lightly coat the roes in seasoned flour and cook in the butter until brown and firm to the touch (approx. 5mins. on each side), remove from pan and keep warm. Add the remaining butter to the pan juices and when melted and changing colour add the balsamic vinegar and stir before removing from heat. Place the cooked roes on a bed of mixed salad leaves set on individual plates. Pour the sauce over the roes and scatter with freshly chopped parsley. Serve with brown bread and butter.

Lazy Cook tips – herring roes I think are a most neglected ingredient. They are inexpensive and available throughout the winter months. Quick and easy to prepare they have a unique flavour and texture. This is one of the many ways in which I serve them.

Mediterranean Tart served with a Last-Minute Tomato Sauce

serves 6-8
175gms (6ozs) brown or white bread – break into pieces
1 desst. mixed fresh herbs (or 1 teas. dried)
1 large egg
1 lemon – juice and zest
freshly ground pepper
1 large red onion – skin and slice into rings
1 x 200gm jar sundried tomatoes in oil
Last-Minute Tomato Sauce (recipe page 12)

Put the bread and herbs into a food processor and process until they crumb. Add the egg, lemon juice and freshly ground pepper and process to a sticky consistency. Set oven at gas 4/400°F/200°C/Aga baking oven. Heat one tablespoon of oil from the jar of sundried tomatoes, add the onion rings, place lid on pan and cook until the onions begin to soften. Lightly oil the base and sides of a shallow ovenproof pie or flan dish and cover the surface with the cooked onion rings, top with the sundried tomatoes (drained from the oil), then spread the processed mixture on top and press down. Bake in the pre-set oven for 20-30mins. Remove from oven and loosen the sides using a palette knife before turning on to a serving dish. Serve with a Last-Minute Tomato Sauce.

Lazy Cook tips – the processed mixture should be of a sticky consistency. If it appears too dry add a little cold water; if it is too moist add a few more breadcrumbs. To reduce the fat content of this recipe, soften the onion rings in a little boiling water. This is a very colourful and tasty tart to serve as a starter, a light lunch or supper dish.

Last-Minute Tomato Sauce

6 tbls. tomato ketchup
1 teas. Worcestershire sauce
a few spots tabasco
1 teas. fresh lemon juice
good pinch basil – fresh or dried
good pinch sugar

Whisk all ingredients in a pan and bring to a simmer. Adjust seasoning to suit your palate. Serve hot, warm or cold. Store in a covered container in a fridge or cold larder for future use. Use within 5 days.

Mussels wrapped in Bacon served on a bed of Noodles with a Marmalade Pickle

to serve 4
12 large cooked mussels
6 rashers streaky bacon – without rind
2 shallots – skin and finely chop
cooked egg noodles
Marmalade Pickle (recipe page 13)

Set oven at gas 6/450°F/220°C/Aga roasting oven. Wrap each mussel in half a rasher of streaky bacon, put on a skewer and bake for 10-15mins. turning half-way through baking. To serve in individual portions, place some of the cooked noodles in the centre of a hot serving dish, put three mussel rolls on top and pour a little of the marmalade pickle over, serve any remaining pickle separately.

Lazy Cook tips – large cooked mussels are available from supermarkets and delicatessens. Cook under a grill if it is more convenient. Cook the noodles following the manufacturer's instructions.

Marmalade Pickle

2 shallots – skin and finely chop
2 teas. wine vinegar
2 tbls. orange marmalade
freshly round pepper
a good pinch ground clove

Soften the shallots in a little boiling water, with lid on pan. Stir in the marmalade, vinegar, pepper and ground clove and bring to a simmer. Taste and add a little more wine vinegar to sharpen the flavour if necessary.

Lazy Cook tips – this pickle is another of those useful ingredients to have in store. It can be stored in a covered jar in a fridge or cold larder.

Parsnip and Ginger Soup

serves 4
1 large onion – chop
1 large parsnip – quarter and slice
squeeze of fresh lemon juice
600ml (1pt) stock
2 teas. sundried tomato purée
1 teas. grated ginger
several pinches of mixed herbs
freshly ground pepper
a little single cream to finish – optional

Soften the prepared onion and parsnip in a little boiling water and lemon juice, with lid on pan.   Add all remaining ingredients (except the cream), bring to a simmer and simmer with lid on pan for 20-30mins.   Using a slotted spoon, put the solid ingredients into a food processor or liquidiser and process to a purée.   Return to the pan and stir in a little cream.   Test for seasoning and adjust if necessary before serving.

Lazy Cook tips – stir in a little more stock if the finished soup is too thick. For an alternative presentation, swirl a little cream on to each portion and garnish with a little finely chopped parsley.   If you cook by Aga the simmering process should be done in the simmering oven.   Serve with hot bread or rolls.   A good winter soup for family or for entertaining.

Pumpkin Soup

serves 6-8
450gms (1 lb) pumpkin flesh – cut into small pieces
225gms (8ozs) potatoes – peel and cut into small pieces
225gms (8ozs) onions – skin and chop
1 ltr (1¾pts) water
1 x 230gm tin tomatoes
freshly ground pepper
½ teas. herbes de Provence
1 teas. Dijon mustard
1 oz single cream
chopped chives for garnish

Remove all seeds, centre pithy flesh and skin from the pumpkin before weighing and cutting into small pieces.   Put all ingredients (except the cream and chives) into a large pan, cover with cold water and bring to boil, skim the top, cover and simmer until the vegetables have softened (this can take three-quarters to one hour).   Using a slotted spoon put the vegetables into a food processor or liquidiser and process until smooth, return to the pan and bring back to simmer, stir in the single cream and serve adding a few chopped chives to each serving.

Lazy Cook tips – the colour of this soup is golden and the flavour is wholesome, just perfect for serving round a bonfire. Pumpkin absorbs a lot of liquid and if the consistency of the soup is too thick add more stock, or hot water mixed with a little tomato purée. If an Aga user the simmering process should be done in the simmering oven. Make in advance of serving and store, covered, in a fridge or cold larder.

Main Courses

Baked Bean Pie

1 leek (or large onion) – slice
mushrooms – chopped or sliced
cooked sausages – slice
left over pieces of cooked bacon, ham or chicken
1 large tin of baked beans
100ml (4fl.ozs) milk
garlic
freshly ground white pepper
mushroom ketchup
Worcestershire sauce
A few pinches dried herbs
tomato purée
mashed potato
cheese – grated

Slightly soften the prepared leek in a little boiling water with lid on pan. Stir in the remaining ingredients (except the mashed potato and grated cheese) and put into an ovenproof dish. Cover with mashed potato and scatter with grated cheese. Heat under a grill or in a hot oven (gas 6/450°F/220°C/Aga roasting oven) until crisp and brown on top. Serve with hot bread

Lazy Cook tips – the quantities in this recipe vary depending on the numbers of people being served and the amounts of left-over ingredients available. The mashed potato can be prepared using fresh potatoes or a packet of dried. The cheese topping is optional, if not used brush the potato with beaten egg or melted butter. Very quick to make, very filling and very popular with children of all ages.

Mashed Potato – peel and cut potatoes into pieces before boiling until soft. Strain off liquid, add a little milk, a good nut of butter and several gratings of nutmeg and mash until smooth.

Baked Cod with Oyster Mushrooms

serves 4
1 large fillet of cod
2 tbls. fresh or dried breadcrumbs (brown or white)
a nut of butter
100gms (4ozs) oyster mushrooms – wipe with damp kitchen roll
100ml (4fl.ozs) white wine
a few spots mushroom ketchup
1 tbls. single cream

Set oven at gas 6/450°F/220°C/Aga roasting oven.
Place the fish in a lightly oiled shallow ovenproof dish, skin side down.
Top with breadcrumbs and shavings of butter and bake for 10-20mins. in
the pre-set oven.   Heat the wine and mushroom ketchup in a large pan,
add the mushrooms and gently simmer, with lid on pan, for 5mins.   Stir in
the cream and season with freshly ground white pepper, keep warm.   To
serve, arrange the mushrooms down the centre of the fish and serve the
sauce separately.

*Lazy Cook tips – the baking time will depend on the thickness of the cod, a
large fillet, or individual portions can be baked.   Use double cream for a
richer sauce.*

Baked Mackerel Fillets with a Leek and Tomato Sauce served on a bed of Nutty Brown Rice

serves 4
4 fresh mackerel fillets
1 leek
100gms (4ozs) mushrooms – wipe with damp kitchen roll, and slice
1 x 400gm tin chopped tomatoes
1 teas. tomato purée
50ml (2fl.ozs) stock or water
a dash of wine – red or white
a pinch of sugar
several good pinches mixed dried herbs
freshly ground white pepper
a handful of pitted black olives
freshly chopped parsley
boiled rice (recipe on page 123)

Set oven at gas 6/450°F/220°C/Aga roasting oven.
Put a film of cold water in a shallow ovenproof dish and add the fillets, skin side down, bake in the pre-set oven for 4-5mins. or until firm to the touch, remove from oven and keep warm.   Top and tail and thinly slice the leek, wash under a cold running tap then cook for a minute in a little boiling water, with lid on pan.   Add all remaining ingredients (except the parsley and rice) and simmer for a few minutes.   To serve, spread the cooked rice over the base of a large hot serving dish and place the baked mackerel on top.   Bring the sauce back to a simmer, spoon a little over the mackerel and serve the remainder separately.

Lazy Cook tips – a good fishmonger or supermarket will fillet fresh mackerel for you.   These fillets can be baked in the oven or cooked in a microwave.   This is a very colourful dish to serve and everything about this recipe is healthy eating.

Daube – a casserole to be prepared a day or two before serving

serves 6-8
900gms (2lbs) lean stewing steak – cut into mouthsized pieces
2 medium sized onions – skin and thinly slice
225gms (8ozs) carrots – scrub and thinly slice
2 garlic cloves – crushed
2 bayleaves – crumbled
2 teas. dried oregano (or mixed herbs)
freshly ground black pepper
300ml (½pt) wine – red or white
2 tbls. extra virgin olive oil
225gms (8ozs) rindless streaky bacon – cut into pieces
225gms (8ozs) mushooms – wipe and slice
1 x 400gm tin chopped tomatoes
pinch sugar
50gms (2ozs) plain flour
600ml (1pt) stock

To prepare – put the meat, onions, carrots, garlic, bayleaves, mixed herbs and pepper, wine and oil into a bowl and stir well.   Cover and leave in a fridge or cold larder to marinade for 24hrs. stirring occasionally.

To cook - layer the marinaded ingredients (drained from the juices), with the mushrooms, tomatoes and sugar, into a large casserole ending with the marinaded ingredients on top.   Mix the flour to a paste with a little cold water, add this, and the stock, to the marinaded juices and stir over a gentle heat until it boils.   Pour over the casserole ingredients, cover and put into a hot oven (gas 6/450°F/220°C/Aga roasting oven) for 10mins. then lower the temperature to gas 3/300°F/150°C/Aga simmering oven and cook for 2-3hrs. or until the meat is tender.   Serve hot or cold.

Lazy Cook tips – once cooked this casserole can be kept for several days. Store, covered, in a fridge or cold larder before serving.   It has an excellent flavour.

Devilled Sausages in Pitta Parcels

to make 4
1 tbls. fresh lemon juice
1tbls. Worcestershire sauce
good pinch cayenne pepper
1 teas. made mustard
1 teas. tomato ketchup
1 teas. soured cream
4 cooked sausages – cut into pieces
4 pitta breads

Make a sauce by simmering all the ingredients (except the sausages and pitta bread) in a pan then stir in the sausage pieces. Bake the pitta bread as instructed by the manufacturer, make a slit at the top of each and fill with the sausage mixture.

Lazy Cook tips – these are so quick to prepare and easy to handle – ideal for serving around a bonfire. Use gamey sausages for the best flavour. Add a little more cream if the flavour is too hot for your palate. Serve wrapped in a paper serviette.

Lambs Liver with Onion Pasta

serves 4
450gms (1 lb) lambs liver –sliced
1 tbls flour seasoned with freshly ground pepper
a little lamb dripping, (or oil)
450gms (1 lb) onions – skin and slice into rings
fresh rosemary – chop
150ml (¼pt) white wine
2 teas. grain mustard
fresh lemon juice
cooked pasta – follow the manufacturer's cooking instructions

Dry the liver slices on kitchen roll. Heat a little dripping (or oil) in a pan, lightly coat the liver slices in the seasoned flour and cook in the hot fat (about a minute on each side). Remove from pan and keep warm. Scrape up the pan juices and add a little more dripping or oil and when hot add the onion rings and rosemary and cook until the onions begin to soften, remove from pan and keep warm Stir the wine into the pan juices and boil until reduced a little. Add the mustard, onion rings and cooked pasta and stir until hot. To serve, put the pasta mixture on to a large hot serving dish, arrange the cooked liver slices on top and moisten with fresh lemon juice.

Lazy Cook tips – liver slices are cooked when the blood seeps out. They take between 30 secs. to 1 min. on each side, depending on the thickness of the slices. Avoid overcooking - this will toughen the liver and spoil its delicate flavour.

Pork Fillet with Sundried Tomatoes and Black Olives

serves 4
1 large pork fillet
a little flour seasoned with freshly ground pepper
oil
2 shallots – skin and finely chop
150ml (¼pt) white wine
150ml (¼pt) stock
1 teas. sundried tomato purée
1 jar sundried tomatoes in oil
100gms (4ozs) pitted black olives
pinch of sugar

Set oven at as gas 6/450°F/220°C/Aga roasting oven.

Trim off any excess fat or gristle before slicing the fillet into lengths. Heat 2 tbls. oil in a shallow pan, coat the slices in the seasoned flour and cook for a minute or two on each side in the oil then transfer to a shallow ovenproof dish. Scrape up the juices from the base of the pan, pour in a little water, add the shallots and cook until softened, with lid on pan. Add the wine and stock and boil to reduce a little. Stir in the tomato purée, sundried tomatoes and olives, season with a pinch of sugar and a little freshly ground pepper before pouring over the pork slices. Cover and bake for 10mins in the pre-set oven then reduce the temperature to gas 3/300°F/150°C/Aga simmering oven, and bake for a further 20mins. or until the pork is cooked before serving.

Lazy Cook tips – this recipe can be prepared a day or two in advance and reheated to serve. Store, covered, in a fridge or cold larder. The combined flavours are excellent and the colours attractive. Use the oil from the jar of sundried tomatoes for the initial sealing of the fillet slices, it will add to the good flavours.

Ratatouille Bake

serves 6-8
225gms (8ozs) self-raising flour
100gms (4ozs) margarine – cut into pieces
75ml (2-3fl.ozs) milk
ratatouille (recipe on page 23)
100gms (4ozs) strong cheddar cheese
50gms (2ozs) chopped walnuts
50gms (2ozs) jumbo oats

Set oven at gas 6/450°F/220°C/Aga roasting oven.

Put the flour and margarine into a food processor and process for a few seconds before pouring in the milk until a smooth dough is formed. Roll out to fit a large, lightly oiled, ovenproof plate, or swiss roll tin. Cover with the ratatouille (draining off excess liquid). Mix the cheese, walnuts and oats together and scatter over the top. Bake for 20-30mins. Slice to serve, hot or cold.

Lazy Cook tips – if this is baked in a swiss roll tin, shape the dough up the sides of the tin to form a case in which to hold the filling. Tinned ratatouille can be used, drain off excess liquid before adding to the base. This liquid can be heated and served as a sauce, or added to soup.

Ratatouille

1 large onion – skin and slice
1 aubergine – top, tail and slice
1 green pepper – remove stalk and seeds, slice pepper
1 x 400gm. tin chopped tomatoes
garlic – optional
pinch sugar
freshly ground pepper
several good pinches mixed dried herbs

Soften the onion in a little boiling water with lid on pan. Add all remaining ingredients, place lid on pan and simmer for 30-45mins. or until all the vegetables have softened. Serve as a vegetable accompaniment to meat or fish, or in a vegetarian recipe.

Lazy Cook tips – to enrich the flavour, add a little red wine before simmering. Ratatouille is one of those really useful ingredients to have in store in winter. It will keep, covered, in a fridge or cold larder for several days, or can be frozen. Because of the protein content of the aubergine, it is extremely useful if catering for vegetarians and it can be presented in so many different ways. Any that remains will add flavour to a soup.

Roasts

Sunday Roast

To me there is something very special about a "Sunday" roast and they never taste as good if served any other day. Today's lifestyle has brought about many changes in our eating habits but, if you are able to gather the family and friends together on Sundays a roast is still the quickest and simplest of meals to serve. All cuts of meat for roasting need a little preparation before cooking and the following points may help to avoid disappointment –

Allow the chosen joint to come to room temperature before it is put into the oven. Wipe it with damp kitchen paper and weigh.

Roasting times vary according to the chosen joint, the size, and desired texture when cooked, i.e. eaten red, pink or well done – refer to recipes for individual joints. Add to the estimated roasting time an extra 20mins. "resting time" after it leaves the oven and before it is carved. This resting time is necessary to allow the juices which have risen during cooking to fall back into the joint and keep it moist.

Always place the joint on a meat trivet in a roasting tin to cook.

Always put the prepared joint into a hot oven to seal in the flavour.

Roast Beef

Allow 20mins. per 450gms (1 lb) plus 15mins. - for well done
    "   20mins. per 450gms (1 lb)   for medium rare
    "   15mins. per 450gms (1 lb)   - for cooked rare

Set oven at gas 6/450°F/220°C/Aga roasting oven.
Smear a little dripping on to the base of the roasting tin before adding the joint, placed on a meat trivet. Top the joint with a piece of beef fat (or with beef dripping) and put into the pre-set oven. Thirty minutes before the joint is ready to be removed from the oven pour a Yorkshire Pudding batter into the tin (recipe on page 25).

Remove the joint at the estimated cooking time leaving the Yorkshire Pudding to become crisp at the edges but soggy in the middle. To serve, put the joint on to a large serving dish and surround with pieces of Yorkshire Pudding.

Accompany with horseradish sauce and English mustard. Because the Yorkshire Pudding has taken up the pan juices, I make gravy to accompany roast beef in a separate pan (recipe on page 29).

Yorkshire Pudding Batter

serves 4-6
100gms (4ozs) plain flour
300ml (½ pt) milk
2 large eggs

Put the flour into a food processor or liquidiser and process for a few seconds, add the milk and eggs and process until smooth. Pour into a jug, cover, and store in a fridge or cold larder for one hour. Before cooking whisk in approximately 2ozs cold water taken from a running tap, then pour into the roasting tin.

Lazy Cook tips – the batter should be made an hour before it is cooked, this allows the starch grains in the flour to swell and thicken the batter. The addition of cold water will thin it and lighten it as it cooks. Individual Yorkshire Puddings can be baked in patti tins containing a little hot fat, but I prefer it baked beneath the joint where it collects the meat juices adding a wonderful flavour. I serve plain boiled potatoes with roast beef, a good contrast, I think, to the richness of the meat and Yorkshire Pudding.

Roast Chicken

Set oven at gas 6/450°F/220°C/Aga roasting oven.
Weigh the chicken and allow 20mins. per 450gms (1 lb) roasting time.
Put the chicken on a meat trivet in a roasting tin and add approx. 600ml
(1pt) hot water. Smear the breasts and legs with butter and roast in the
pre-set oven for 30mins. Remove from oven and reduce the temperature
to gas 4/400°F/200°C/Aga baking oven. Cover with foil to seal in the
steam, return to the oven and continue roasting for the estimated time.
Test that the chicken is cooked by piercing the thickest part of the leg with
a match-stick, if the juices run clear it is cooked, if they run pink longer
cooking time is needed. When cooked, remove from the oven, loosen the
foil and allow the chicken to rest for 20mins. before transferring it to a hot
serving dish ready for carving. Make gravy using the juices in the
roasting tin (recipe on page 29).

*Lazy Cook tips – I prefer this "steam-roasting" method of roasting a
chicken - it produces a more moist flesh. Take care when loosening the
foil as hot steam escapes and can scald you. If all the pan juices (stock),
are not used for gravy, pour them into a basin and when cold store in a
fridge for future use. Use within 4 days after which remove any surface
fat and discard, put the stock into a freezer bag and freeze (advice on stock
making on page 125).*

*If you are few in number and a whole roast chicken is too much, before
cooking, cut the skin and pull back, remove the breasts which can be
frozen for future use. Fill the breast cavities with bacon rolls and cocktail
sausages, cover with the skin and secure with a skewer, roast as a whole
chicken.*

Roast Lamb

Allow 20mins. per 450gms (1 lb) - cooked pink
      30mins. "   "   "   - well cooked

Set oven at gas 6/450°F/220°C/Aga roasting oven.
Stand the joint on a meat trivet in a roasting tin and add approximately 600ml (1pt) hot water before putting into the pre-set oven, and after 20mins. reduce the oven temperature to gas 4/400°F/200°C/Aga baking oven.   When cooked remove from oven and allow to rest for 20mins. before transferring to a hot serving dish ready for carving.   Serve mint sauce, mint or redcurrant jelly, with roast lamb.

Lazy Cook tips – if a whole or a half shoulder is too much for your immediate needs, remove the fillet and freeze for future use.

Roast Pork

Pork should always be well cooked – allow 45mins. per 450gms (1 lb).

Set oven at gas 6/450°F/220°C/Aga roasting oven.
For a crisp crackling, dry the rind with kitchen roll, brush it with oil and scatter liberally with salt.   Pour in a little boiling water to cover the base of the roasting tin before adding the prepared joint, standing it on a meat trivet. Put into pre-set oven and after 30mins. reduce the oven temperature to gas 4/400°F/200°C/Aga baking oven for the remainder of the roasting time.   Test that it is cooked by piercing the centre, or the thickest part of the joint, with a metal skewer and if the juices run clear it is cooked; if they run pink, cook for a little longer and test again.   Serve with apple sauce (recipe on page 121), sage and onion stuffing (recipe on page 28), or English mustard.

Lazy Cook tips – the rind will only become crisp if it is dry before the oil and salt are added; it should then be put immediately into a hot oven.   It is very important that pork is well cooked, continue testing until the juices run clear.

Sage and Onion Stuffing

1 large onion – skin and chop
220 gms (8ozs) fresh breadcrumbs – brown or white
2 teas. dried sage (or about 20 fresh sage leaves)

Soften the prepared onion in approximately 300ml (½pt) boiling water, with lid on pan. Add the breadcrumbs and sage and stir well before packing into a lightly oiled, shallow, ovenproof dish. Leave for 20mins. before baking for 20-30mins. at gas 4/400°F/200°C/Aga baking oven. Serve hot or cold.

Lazy Cook tips – the consistency should be sticky when all the ingredients are mixed. Add more hot water if it is too dry, or more breadcrumbs if it is too wet. Store after cooking, covered, in a fridge or cold larder, use within 5 days.

Roast Vegetables

To prepare –

Onions – skin small onions and leave whole.

Parsnips – top and tail before scrubbing the skin. Cut into quarter lengths.

Potatoes – peel and cut into pieces. Leave in cold water once peeled.

To roast – set oven at gas 6/450°F/220°C/Aga roasting oven.
Par boil the prepared vegetables by putting into a pan, cover with cold water and bring to the boil, remove from heat and strain off the cooking liquid. Heat one tablespoon oil in a shallow ovenproof dish and add the vegetables coating them in the hot oil. Put into the pre-set oven for 45mins. to 1 hr or until brown and crisp.

Lazy Cook tips – once coated in the hot fat the vegetables can be left for a few hours before roasting. Very little oil is needed to brown the vegetables. Use the cooking liquid to boil other vegetables and finally to add to the gravy.

Roast Pumpkin – remove and discard the seeds, centre pithy flesh and skin from the pumpkin and cut it into slices. Heat 1-2tbls. oil in a shallow ovenproof dish, add the prepared pumpkin slices and coat with the hot oil. Sprinkle a little ground clove on each slice and bake in a hot oven until soft and beginning to brown (about one hour). Serve with a roast.

Lazy Cook tips – this, I think, is one of the most delicious ways of serving pumpkin, the flavour is sweet and so good.

Gravy - *to serve with a roast*

Add approx. 50gms (2ozs) plain flour to a little cold water and mix to a smooth paste. Pour this into the roasting tin after the joint has been removed, add vegetable stock, stir and bring to a boil scraping up any bits which may have settled on the base of the roasting tin. Add a few spots of gravy browning and boil for about 2 mins. or until it thickens. Add more vegetable stock if it is too thick.

Lazy Cook tips – a little wine (red or white), redcurrant or mint jelly, cranberry sauce or marmalade are just a few individual ingredients which can be added to gravy at the boiling stage to give different flavours.

Savoury Pumpkin Flan

serves 6-8
450gms (1 lb) pumpkin flesh – cut into small pieces
1 medium sized cooking apple
300ml (½pt) water
freshly ground white pepper
a good pinch ground clove
a good pinch ground cinnamon
50gms (2ozs) Gruyere cheese – grated
1 tbls. cream (optional)
1 medium sized onion – skin and slice into rings
1 tbls. oil
1 cooked pastry case

Prepare the pumpkin by removing all the seeds, centre pithy flesh and skin before weighing the required amount and cutting it into small pieces. Skin, core and chop the apple. Put the prepared pumpkin, apple and water into a pan, bring to a simmer and simmer, with lid on pan until the pumpkin has softened, stirring occasionally and adding a little more water if necessary. Remove from the heat and stir in the pepper, clove, cinnamon, cheese and cream and put into the cooked pastry case. Heat the oil in a pan, add the onion rings, place lid on pan and cook until the rings begin to soften, arrange over the pumpkin mixture in the flan case. Bake at gas 6/450°F/220°C/Aga roasting oven for about 10mins. or until the onions begin to brown. Serve hot.

Lazy Cook tips – pumpkin absorbs a lot of water and more may need to be added during the simmering process, when cooked it should resemble a purée texture. I serve this flan with crispy bacon and a Last-Minute Tomato Sauce (recipe on page 12).

Spicy Chicken

serves 4-6
1 ring of black pudding – remove skin
450gms (1 lb) cooked chicken
100ml (4ozs) chicken stock
100ml (4ozs) white wine
1 tin Campbells condensed mushroom soup
150ml (¼pt) single cream

Set oven at gas 6/450°F/220°C/Aga roasting oven. Slice the black pudding and arrange over the base of a shallow ovenproof dish. Break the chicken into pieces and put over the black pudding. Boil the stock and wine until they reduce by half, stir in the soup and cream and bring to a simmer, pour over the chicken, cover with foil, place on a baking sheet and reheat until hot and bubbly in the pre-set oven. Serve with rice and vegetables.

Lazy Cook tips – this recipe is equally good made with turkey pieces. It can be prepared in advance and reheated to serve. Store, covered, in a fridge or larder.

Tuna Steaks with a Mustard and Caper Cream sauce

serves 4
4 tuna steaks
a little oil
freshly ground pepper
1 tbls. capers
mustard and caper cream sauce (recipe below)

Heat a large frying or sauté pan.   Brush the steaks on each side with oil and season with a little freshly ground pepper.   Cook in the hot pan, 2mins. each side.   Scrape up the pan juices and add the mustard cream sauce ingredients and the capers and whisk until boiling.   Serve the steaks with a little sauce poured over each.   Serve the remainder separately.

Lazy Cook tips – it is important not to overcook tuna as it becomes very dry and loses its delicate flavour.   This is one of the quickest meals I prepare, serve it hot or cold.

Mustard and Caper Cream Sauce

1 teas. Dijon mustard
1 teas. grain mustard
1 teas. sundried tomato purée
2 teas. capers
1 tbls. double cream
150ml (¼pt) stock – vegetable, chicken or fish

Put all ingredients into a pan and whisk together until boiling.   Serve hot or cold.

Lazy Cook tips – this is one of the quickest sauces I make and is an excellent example of the use of store-cupboard ingredients.   When cold store in a covered container in a fridge or cold larder.   Vary the flavours by replacing the capers with cocktail onions, chopped anchovies or herbs – this recipe is a must in a Lazy Cook's repertoire.

Puddings

Apple Charlotte

serves 6-8
700gms (1½ lbs) bramley apples
75gms (3ozs) shredded suet
75gms (3ozs) demerera sugar
175gms (6ozs) dried breadcrumbs – brown or white (recipe on page 111)
1 lemon – juice and rind

Set oven at gas 6/450°F/220°C/Aga roasting oven.
Peel, core and chop the apples.   Mix the suet, sugar, breadcrumbs and lemon rind together.   Lightly oil a deep pie dish and fill with layers of apple and breadcrumb mixture, starting with the apples and ending with the breadcrumbs.   Pour lemon juice over the top and bake for 20-30mins. Serve hot with custard or cream.

Lazy Cook tips – the use of dried breadcrumbs gives this Charlotte a lightness of texture.   Add more lemon juice if you enjoy a really strong lemon flavour.   A delicious pudding and so quick to make.

Bitter Chocolate Mousse with Roasted Hazelnuts

serves 6
100gms (4 ozs) bitter chocolate
50gms (2 ozs) butter
4 size 1 eggs – separated
50gms (2 ozs) roasted hazelnuts – chopped (recipe on page 33)
2 tbls. hazelnut liqueur
150ml (¼pt) double cream
for decoration – grated bitter chocolate
                 chopped hazelnuts

Melt the chocolate and butter together and allow to cool a little before stirring in the egg yolks, chopped hazelnuts and liqueur. Whip the cream to a soft peak and stir in. Whisk the egg whites until stiff and stir in. Pour into one large or several individual serving dishes and leave in a fridge or cold larder to set. To serve, scatter the top with a mixture of grated bitter chocolate and chopped hazelnuts.

Lazy Cook tips – do not whip the cream too thickly or whisk the egg whites too stiffly. Brandy can be used in place of hazelnut liqueur or, to add a mocha flavour, mix a teaspoon of coffee granules with a tablespoon of hot water and when dissolved stir this into the chocolate mixture.

Roast Hazelnuts – put whole hazelnuts on a swiss roll tin and brown under a grill or in a hot oven (the top of an Aga roasting oven). When the skins have darkened, remove from oven and allow to cool a little before rubbing them off. Store in an airtight jar.

Blackcurrant Crumble

serves 6-8
1 x 680gm jar blackcurrants in syrup
225gms (8ozs) plain flour
100gms (4ozs) butter
75gms (3ozs) demerera sugar

Set oven at gas 6/450°F/220°C/Aga roasting oven.
Put all the blackcurrants and about half of the syrup into a shallow ovenproof dish. Put the flour and one tablespoon sugar into a food processor and process for a few seconds, add the butter (cut into pieces) and process until a breadcrumb texture. Spread this over the blackcurrants and scatter the remaining sugar on top. Stand the dish on a baking tray and bake in the pre-set oven for 15-20mins. or until hot and bubbly. Serve hot or cold with the remaining syrup, single cream or ice-cream.

Lazy Cook tips – this is such an easy pudding and I often serve it after a Sunday roast. Put the blackcurrants in the dish and have the crumble ingredients processed then it can very quickly be put together and put in the oven to bake while the main course is being eaten.   It may be necessary to reduce the oven temperature after 20 minutes to gas 4/400°F/200°C/Aga baking oven.   A really delicious pudding.

Bramble Meringue Pie

serves 6-8
1 ready baked pastry case
450gms (1 lb) bramley cooking apples – peel, core and slice
225gms (8ozs) blackberries – wash
sugar to taste
topping – 2 egg whites
　　　　100gms (4ozs) caster sugar
　　　　a few spots pink food colouring

Set oven at gas 6/450°F/220°C/Aga roasting oven.
Cook the apples and blackberries over a gentle heat with lid on pan, add sugar to taste and leave to cool a little while making the meringue. Whisk the egg whites with a few spots of pink food colouring, until stiff and dry (of a cottonwool texture), then fold in the caster sugar.   Fill the flan case with the cooked apple and blackberry mixture and cover with the meringue.   Bake in the pre-set oven until the meringue begins to brown. Serve warm or cold with single cream.

Lazy Cook tips – the flavours of this pudding are excellent. It can be baked in the hot oven and when the meringue begins to brown the temperature can be reduced to gas 3/300°fF/150°C/Aga simmering oven to allow the meringue to become more crisp.   As a Lazy Cook I always keep a store of ready baked flan cases, these are available from most delicatessens or supermarkets.   With such ingredients to hand the pudding is made in minutes.

Bread Pudding with an Orange and Ginger Wine Sauce

I well remember the bread pudding my Mother made and which I loved. My recipe is, I think, equally delicious but it is much quicker to make. The ginger wine sauce makes it a very special pudding to serve on all occasions.

Serves 6
100gms (4ozs) fresh breadcrumbs (brown or white)
100ml (4ozs) milk
1 desst. black treacle
1 tbls. marmalade
25gms (1oz) shredded suet
½ teas. mixed spice
100gms (4ozs) dried apricots – sliced
Orange and Ginger Wine sauce (recipe below)

Heat the milk, stir in the black treacle and when dissolved add all remaining ingredients and stir well. Pack into a lightly oiled pie dish and leave to rest for 15-30mins. before scattering with a little demerera sugar and baking for 30-40mins. at gas 4/400°F/200°C/Aga baking oven. Serve hot or cold.

Lazy Cook tips – this recipe can also be served as a cake - when cold cut it into chunky pieces. For a more eye-catching presentation, prepare this recipe as follows – smear butter over the base of a pie dish and cover with demerera sugar then arrange the whole apricots on top before covering with the pudding mixture. Bake as directed in the recipe but to serve turn it out on to a hot serving plate. Serve the Ginger Wine Sauce separately.

Orange and Ginger Wine Sauce

1 fresh orange – grated zest and juice
1 teas. orange flower water (optional)
50ml (2ozs) ginger wine

Simmer all the ingredients together for a few minutes. Serve at once or prepare in advance and reheat to serve.

Lazy Cook tips – this is a delicious sauce to serve with many puddings or ice-cream. It can be stored, in a covered container in a fridge or cold larder. Orange flower water is a useful ingredient to have in store and can be added to many cake and pudding recipes, it has a most delicate flavour. Buy from some supermarkets and most delicatessens.

Chocolate Bombe *– a pudding to keep in store*

serves 6-8
to be prepared and frozen –
300ml (½pt) double cream
175gms (6ozs) bitter chocolate
50gms (2ozs) butter
50gms (2ozs) walnuts – chopped
4 size 1 eggs – separated
for decoration (not needed until the pudding is to be served) –
300ml (½pt) double cream
chocolate squares or lace (recipe on page 37)

To prepare – whip the cream to a spreadable consistency and stir in approx. 50gms (2ozs) of the chocolate, grated. Spread this to cover the inside of a 1 ltr (2pt) basin, put into a freezer bag and freeze. Melt the remaining chocolate and butter together, allow to cool a little before stirring in the egg yolks and the walnuts. Whisk the egg whites to a stiff consistency and stir into the chocolate mixture, pour this into the frozen cream mould and refreeze for a minimum of 24hrs. To serve, remove from the freezer and allow to begin to thaw before loosening from the basin using a palette knife. Turn it on to a serving dish and spread or pipe with whipped cream and spike with chocolate squares or lace.

Lazy Cook tips – allow the pudding to begin to thaw in the fridge for about one hour after which remove it from the basin and return to fridge to thaw completely, test by sticking a skewer into it. I promise you it will not collapse when thawed. This is a most useful pudding to have in store. If you have over-bought cream, line a basin as described in the recipe and freeze. The centre filling can be added at a later date. For a special occasion, stick sparklers into the bombe and light before carrying to the table – remove the sparklers before serving.

Chocolate Lace

Pipe melted chocolate on to foil, pipe an outer shape and fill in the centre with piped squiggles. When set, store on the foil in a box, ease off the foil with a knife to use.

Chocolate Squares

Spread melted chocolate on to a piece of foil and allow to set before cutting into squares. Make in advance and store in a box.

Lemon Meringue Gateau

serves 8-10
2 meringue plates (recipe below)
lemon curd
1 lemon – juice and rind
300ml (½pt) double cream – whip to a spreading consistency

Stir a tablespoon of lemon juice into 4tbls. of the lemon curd and spread this over the base of a meringue plate then spread with half of the whipped cream. Top with the second meringue plate and spread the remaining cream on top. Heat a tablespoon of lemon curd in a small pan until it becomes runny and using a teaspoon trail this in lines across the cream then scatter with lemon zest. Leave in a fridge or cold larder for several hours before serving.

Lazy Cook tips – I assemble this pudding directly on to a serving plate securing the base meringue with a tablespoon of whipped cream. If the cream is accidently overwhipped, "very gently" stir in a tablespoon or two of milk and it should return to a smooth consistency. This pudding is best made several hours before it is served, the flavour is excellent. With all ingredients to hand, it can be assembled in minutes – very Lazy Cook.

Meringue Plates

to make 2 x 25cms (10") in diameter
4 size 1 egg whites
225gms (8ozs) caster sugar
pinch cream of tartare

Set oven at gas 2/200°F/100°C/Aga simmering oven.

Cover 2 baking trays with household parchment or bake-o-glide. Whisk the egg whites until they are stiff and dry (of a cottonwool texture). Whisk or fold in the sugar and cream of tartare and spread the mixture equally on to the prepared baking trays in rounds approx. 25cms (10") in diameter. Place in the pre-set oven to dry (this can take between 2 and 4 hours). Take from oven and remove from paper, store in airtight polythene or freezer bags until needed.

Lazy Cook tips – make sure the whites are really stiff before the sugar is added. They are dry when they can be peeled from the paper. A most useful ingredient to have in store. They will remain crisp for at least 2 months.

Norwegian Apples

serves 4-6
1 kilo (2¼lbs) apple purée (recipe on page 121)
300ml (½pt) double cream
1 tbls. crushed biscuit crumbs
1 tbls. bitter chocolate – chopped into pieces
1 tbls. walnuts – chopped into pieces

Pile the apple purée on to a large serving dish. Whip the cream to a soft peak and spread over the purée. Mix the biscuit crumbs, chocolate and walnuts together and scatter over the top, serve.

Poires Belle Hélène

serves 6
1 large ripe pear
600ml (1pt) cold rice pudding (recipe on page 39)
100gms (4ozs) bitter chocolate – grated or chopped
100gms (4ozs) caster sugar

Peel, core and cut the pear into small cubes and put to cover the base of 6 ramekin dishes. Cover with cold rice pudding, then with grated chocolate and finally with a good layer of caster sugar. Place under a hot grill until the sugar has browned. Allow to cool before serving.

Lazy Cook tips – this is my version of the classic Poires Belle Hélène which was so popular in the 1960's. Tinned pears and tinned rice can be used (drain the juices from the pears). If you don't have a grill, brown the sugar using a chefs butane gas torch (follow manufacturer's instructions before use). Once made these little puddings can be stored in a fridge for several days before serving, cover with clingfilm to store. A delicious pudding and one which will surprise your guests as they will think they are being served Crème Brulee.

Traditional Rice Pudding

serves 4
3 desst. pudding rice
1 desst. granulated sugar
600ml (1pt) full cream milk
a nut of butter
freshly grated nutmeg

Set oven at gas 4/400°F/200°C/Aga baking oven.
Wash the rice before putting it into a one pint ovenproof pudding dish. Add all remaining ingredients and stir well. Place on a baking tray and bake for 20-30mins. in the pre-set oven, then reduce the temperature to gas 3/300°F/150°C/Aga simmering oven for a further 1 hr. or until the milk has been absorbed into the rice and the texture is soft and creamy. Serve hot or cold.

Lazy Cook tips – my Mother always added a handful of sultanas to the pudding before it was cooked.

Pumpkin Pie

serves 6-10
450gms (1 lb) pumpkin flesh – cut into mouthsized pieces
1 medium sized bramley apple – peel, core and chop
1 jar mincemeat
a good pinch ground clove
1 ready baked pastry case
topping – 2 x size 1 egg whites
           100gms (4ozs) caster sugar
           several good pinches mixed spice

Prepare the pumpkin by removing all the seeds, centre pithy flesh and skin before weighing the required amount and cutting into small pieces. Put the prepared pumpkin and apple into a pan, cover with cold water and simmer, with lid on pan, until the pumpkin has softened, stirring occcasionally and adding a little more water if necessary. Remove from heat and stir in half a jar of mincemeat and the ground clove, allow to cool a little before putting into the baked pastry case. Set oven at gas 6/450°F/220°C/Aga roasting oven. Make the meringue topping by whisking the egg whites until they are stiff and dry (of a cottonwool consistency). Mix the sugar and spice together and whisk or fold into the whites. Spread this over the top of the pumpkin mixture and bake in the pre-set oven for 10mins. or until the meringue begins to brown. Serve warm or cold with single cream.

Lazy Cook tips – pumpkin absorbs a lot of water, add more as necessary, it should resemble a puree when cooked. The oven temperature can be reduced to gas 3/300°F/150°C/Aga simmering oven once the meringue has browned.

Toffee Apple Pudding

serves 6-8
700gms (1½ lbs) bramley cooking apples
225gms (8ozs) demerera sugar
225gms (8ozs) self-raising flour
several good pinches ground cinnamon
100gms (4ozs) butter
a little icing sugar

Set oven at gas 4/400°F/200°C/Aga baking oven.

Line the base of an 18cms/7" round cake tin with bake-o-glide, or greaseproof well buttered, butter the sides of the tin also. Peel, core and slice the apples into a large bowl and stir in the sugar. Put the flour, cinnamon and butter into a food processor and process until a pastry crumb texture, stir this into the apples. Pack into the prepared tin and bake for 45-60mins. or until brown on top. Loosen the sides with a knife and turn on to a serving plate. Peel off the lining paper and sieve the top with icing sugar. Serve hot, warm or cold with single cream, ice cream or custard.

Lazy Cook tips – for a darker pudding and of a different flavour, use dark cane sugar instead of caster. This is a really quick pudding to make. The longer it is left to bake the more sticky and toffee-like it becomes, reduce the oven temperature to suit your time schedule.

Recommended Menus

Autumn Lunch

Autumn Dinner Party

Sunday Roast

Hallowe'en Party
a fork supper

o o O o o

o o O o o

Cheese and Biscuits

o o O o o

Coffee

Bonfire Party
to be served round the bonfire

The 12 days of Christmas

Since early childhood the atmosphere surrounding Christmas has been exciting and special to me and each year I look forward to the challenge it offers for a little creative cooking – a few of those little luxuries which make Christmas food so memorable. But I also know how daunting it can be when there are so many extra demands on limited time.

"Life is too short to spend unnecessary time in the kitchen." This is the answer I give to everyone who asks my advice on cooking, especially at Christmas. My Lazy Cook recipes will keep everything simple. The tips I give will help you to speed up on the preparation, and the anecdotes are intended to encourage a relaxed attitude.

As with any holiday a little pre-planning is a good idea and the Lazy Cook tips I give will guide you on how far in advance a recipe can be made, stored or frozen.

Index of Recipes page

Starters and Light Meals

Main Courses

Puddings

Starters and Light meals

Baked Avocado with Goats Cheese

serves 4
2 Avocado
Apple purée (recipe on page 121)
4 slices goats cheese

Set oven at gas 6/450°F/220°C/Aga roasting oven.
Cut the avocado in half lengthways and remove the centre stone.　Fill the cavity with apple purée and top with a slice of goats cheese.　Put in an ovenproof dish, or metal tray, and bake in the pre-set oven for 10-15mins.

Lazy Cook tips – to prevent the avocado wobbling about, shave a little of the skin from the base of each halve before filling.　If the avocado is a little unripe, baking will soften it.　Heat under a grill if it is more convenient.　Ready–made apple purée can be used.　Use small avocado if serving as a starter.

Chestnut Paté

100gms (4ozs) dried chestnuts
100gms (4ozs) mushrooms
2 tbls. apple purée (recipe on page 121)
freshly ground pepper
a good pinch ground cloves

Soak the chestnuts in cold water for an hour or two then strain off the liquid and discard.　Put the chestnuts into a pan, cover with fresh water and simmer, with lid on pan, until they soften (approx. 30mins.)　Strain off the liquid and keep. Purée the chestnuts in a food processor or liquidiser.　Soften the mushrooms in a little of the chestnut stock then put into the food processor, add the remaining ingredients and process until smooth.　Serve with toast or rolls.

Lazy Cook tips – the chestnuts can be left to soak overnight.   If the paté is too soft add a few fresh breadcrumbs (brown or white).   If it is too stiff, add a little of the reserved chestnut stock. Store the paté in a covered container in a fridge or cold larder, bring back to room temperature to serve.

Cocktail Blinis with Black Pudding and Brie

cocktail blinis
black pudding – remove skin
brie

Put a slice of black pudding on each blini and cover with brie.   Put on a baking tray and heat under a hot grill, or in a hot oven (gas 6/450°F/220°C/Aga roasting oven).   Serve as a starter garnished with salad leaves drizzled with balsamic vinaigrette (recipe on page 50).   They can also be served with nibbles at a drinks party.

Lazy Cook tips – these can be prepared in advance and heated for serving.

Balsamic Vinaigrette

3 tbls. oil
1 tbls. cider vinegar
1 teas. balsamic vinegar
a little freshly ground pepper

Whisk all together.   Store in a covered container.

Cocktail Blinis with Sardine and Tomato

cocktail blini's
tinned sardines in oil
fresh lemon juice
tomato slices
pinch sugar
freshly ground pepper
mixed dried herbs

Mash the sardines in some of the oil and season with a few squeezes of fresh lemon juice and spread this on to each blini, top with a tomato slice lightly brushed with sardine oil and seasoned with a pinch of sugar, freshly ground pepper and a sprinkling of herbs. Put on a baking tray and heat under a hot grill or in a hot oven (gas 6/450°F/220°C/Aga roasting oven). Serve as a starter garnished with salad leaves, or with nibbles at a drinks party.

Lazy Cook tips – these can be prepared in advance and heated ready for serving. Tinned sardines in tomato can also be used.

Cream of Mushroom Soup

serves 4-6
1 medium sized onion – skin and finely chop
450gms (1 lb) mushrooms – wipe and slice
1 teas. mushroom ketchup
freshly ground white pepper
600ml (1pt) chicken or vegetable stock
300ml (½pt) single cream.

Soften the onion in a little boiling water in a large pan, with lid on. Add the mushrooms and simmer until they begin to soften, with lid on pan. Add the mushroom ketchup, pepper and stock and simmer gently, with lid on pan, for 10-15mins. Using a slotted spoon, remove the onion and mushrooms from the pan and process or liquidise for a few seconds, return to the pan, stir in the cream and bring back to a simmer before serving.

Lazy Cook tips – dark skinned mushrooms will give the soup a good rich colour. A little cream can be swirled on top of each portion as it is served. This soup can be made in advance, store in a covered container in a fridge or cold larder, serve within 4 days. Bring back to a boil and stir in the cream to serve.

Dessert Pear with Smoked Salmon and Peppered Cream

serves 4
2 dessert pears
1 x 80gm pkt peppered Boursin cheese
225gms (8ozs) smoked salmon
4 anchovy fillets
4 thin slices fresh lemon
fresh parsley sprigs
4 thin slices brown bread, buttered and cut into quarters

Skin the pears and cut in half lengthways, remove the stalk and fill the cavity with peppered Boursin and place, cut side down, on individual plates. Cover each pear with strips of smoked salmon and top with a curled anchovy fillet. Garnish the tip of the pear with a lemon slice and a sprig of fresh parsley. Serve with brown bread and butter.

Lazy Cook tips – the combination of these flavours is good. Very quick to prepare and eye-catching in presentation, an excellent starter or light lunch or supper recipe. Additional Boursin can be heated with a little milk to make a runny sauce which can be trailed round each pear. Anchovy fillets can now be purchased from most delicatessen counters, I recommend these in preference to tinned or bottled anchovies. I have used both comice and conference pears in this recipe.

Ham and Tongue Mousse

makes 4-6
175gms (6ozs) ox tongue slices
100gms (4ozs) ham slices – any fat removed
1 teas. made English mustard
4 tbls. single cream
3 teas. cider vinegar
freshly ground white pepper
cranberry sauce
watercress
toast

Break the tongue and ham slices into a food processor or liquidiser, add the mustard, cream, vinegar and pepper and process until a paste is formed.   Put into small pots or ramekins and cover with cranberry sauce. Serve with toast and a garnish of watercress.

Lazy Cook tips – can be made in advance and stored, covered, in a fridge or cold larder.

Leek and Ginger Soup

serves 4
450gms (1 lb) leeks – thinly slice
225gms (8ozs) potatoes – peel and cut into small pieces
1 teas. grated ginger
nutmeg
600ml (1pt) stock
freshly ground pepper
a good squeeze lemon juice
a little single cream – optional

Soften the prepared leeks in a little boiling water with lid on pan. Add all remaining ingredients (except the cream), bring to a simmer and simmer with lid on pan for 20-30mins. or until the potato has softened.   Taste and adjust the seasoning if necessary.   Stir in the cream, bring back to a simmer and serve.

Lazy Cook tips – if a smoother soup is preferred, process or liquidise the solid ingredients when cooked.   Make in advance and store, covered, in a fridge or cold larder.

Party Pizzas

to make 10-12
onions – skin and cut into rings
a little oil
1 French baton or stick
tomato purée
horseradish cream
100gms (4ozs) pitted black olives – roughly cut up
10-12 tomato slices
pinch sugar
mixed herbs
freshly ground pepper
10-12 anchovy fillets
thin slices of cheese – Parmesan, Stilton or Brie

Cook the onions in a little oil until they begin to brown. Cut the bread into 2cms (½") slices and toast on one side only. Mix the tomato puree and horseradish cream together and spread on to the untoasted side of the bread, place on a baking tray, toasted side down. Top each with the cooked onion rings and olives and a tomato slice seasoned with a pinch of sugar, freshly ground pepper and a sprinkling of mixed herbs. Finally add a curled anchovy filled and cover with a slice of cheese. Heat under a grill or in a hot oven (gas 6/450°F/220°C/Aga roasting oven) until hot and bubbly.

Lazy Cook tips – quick to assemble and heat. An ideal party snack served hot and wrapped in a paper serviette. I recommend anchovy fillets available from most delicatessen counters in preference to the tinned or bottled varieties.

Pork Terrine

225gms (8ozs) belly pork – rind removed
450gms (1 lb) diced pork
450gms (1 lb) pork sausagemeat
225gms (8ozs) lambs liver – cut into small pieces
2 tbls. fresh breadcrumbs – brown or white
1 teas. dried thyme and sage – mixed
freshly ground black pepper
1 tbls. cranberry sauce
100ml (4fl.ozs) port
100gms (4ozs) pork dripping – melted
course grain salt

Cut the pork belly into pieces then mix all ingredients together (except the dripping and salt) and leave to marinade for an hour or more. Set oven at gas 3/300°F/150°C/Aga simmering oven. Stir the marinaded ingredients before packing into an ovenproof terrine or pot. Cover and place in a baking tin. Pour in warm water to come half way up the pot (see Bain Marie). Bake for 1 hr. or until firm to the touch. Remove from oven and allow to become cold before covering with a layer of melted dripping to seal. Store in a fridge or cold larder. Bring back to room temperature and scatter the top with course grain salt before serving with toast or bread.

Lazy Cook tips – this terrine can be baked in one large or several smaller pots, or individual ramekins. Adjust the baking time accordingly. A terrine is a good standby to serve as a starter or a light meal, or to serve with an assortment of cold meats.

Tongue Rolls with Mustard Mayonnaise and Blinis

makes 8
8 slices tongue – ox or pork
100gms (4ozs) Roule with Herbe cream cheese
1 tbls. milk
freshly ground black pepper
sprinkling of fresh lemon juice
100gms (4ozs) cooked prawns
chives
watercress
mayonnaise (recipe on page 119)
made English mustard
8 cocktail blinis

Soften the cheese with a little milk and season with freshly ground pepper
and lemon juice.   Spread this on to each tongue slice, top with prawns and
roll up, tie a chive round the middle of each.   Serve on individual plates,
garnished with a little watercress, a spoon of mayonnaise seasoned to taste
with ready made mustard, and a cocktail blini.

*Lazy Cook tips – these rolls can be made in advance and stored, covered,
in a fridge or cold larder, bring back to room temperature before serving.
A colourful and delicious starter, quick and easy to prepare.   Ready-made
mayonnaise can be used.*

Main Courses

Beef Rolls with Apricots and a Black Olive Sauce

makes 4
4 thin slices of lean topside
50gms (2ozs) brandy butter
50gms (2ozs) dried apricots
a little plain flour seasoned with freshly ground white pepper
1 tbls. oil
4 shallots – skin and finely chop
50ml (2fl ozs) red wine
50ml (2fl ozs) stock
50gms (2ozs) pitted black olives – cut up
a good pinch herbes de Provence

Spread each topside slice with brandy butter, top with dried apricots and roll up tightly. Coat each roll in seasoned flour and brown in the hot oil, remove from pan and keep warm. Scrape up the juices from the base of the pan and add the finely chopped shallots, cover and cook over a gentle heat until softened. Add the wine and stock and boil to reduce a little. Return the beef rolls to the pan and spoon a little sauce over each, add the herbes and the olives, bring to a simmer, place lid on pan (or cover with foil), and simmer for 20-30mins. or until the meat is tender. To serve, place the rolls down the centre of a hot serving plate and spoon a little of the sauce over, serve the remaining sauce separately. Serve with potatoes or pasta and a second vegetable of your choice.

Lazy Cook tips – if you cook by Aga the simmering process should be done in the simmering oven. A good recipe to serve at Christmas, a change from the traditional turkey and other seasonal meats.

Duck Breasts served on a bed of Wild and Mixed Rice with a Bitter Orange Sauce

serves 4
4 duck breasts
brown and white rice (recipe on page 123)
wild rice (recipe on page 124)
bunch watercress
bitter orange sauce (recipe below)

Set oven at gas 6/450°F/220°C/Aga roasting oven.
Dry the skins of the breasts, prick all over with a metal skewer and sprinkle liberally with salt. Place them on a meat trivet set in a meat tin with enough cold water to cover the base of the tin. Cook in the pre-set oven for 20-30mins. To serve (on individual hot plates or on one large meat platter), slice each breast, arrange on the mixed rice and coat with a little of the sauce, garnish with watercress. Serve the remaining sauce separately. A quick meal to serve when life is hectic. Full of delicious flavours, colours and textures.

Bitter Orange Sauce

2 shallots – skin and finely chop
2 tbls. bitter orange marmalade
1 x 150ml tin Britvic orange juice
grated zest of one orange

Soften the shallots in a little boiling water, with lid on pan. Stir in the remaining ingredients and simmer for 5 minutes, without lid. Serve hot or cold.

Lazy Cook tips – the sauce can be prepared in advance and reheated, or made while the breasts are cooking. Any remaining sauce can be stored in a covered container in a fridge or cold larder.

Ham with Black Cherry Sauce

serves 4-6
1 ham or bacon joint to serve 4-6 people
2 bayleaves
10 whole cloves
1 tbls. demerera sugar
black cherry sauce (recipe below)

Put the joint in a pan and cover with cold water. Place over a gentle heat and bring slowly to a gentle simmer, without lid. Skim the top then add the bayleaves, cloves and sugar. Place lid on pan and simmer gently for 30mins. to 1 hour depending on the size of the joint. To serve, take the joint from the cooking stock, slice thickly and arrange down the centre of a large hot dish. Cover with a little of the hot sauce including some cherries. Serve with jacket potatoes and a second vegetable of your choice.

Lazy Cook tips – if there is time, allow the joint to soak for an hour or two in cold water before cooking, strain off the soaking water and discard. It is important to bring ham and bacon joints 'slowly' to a simmer and allow them to simmer 'slowly' throughout cooking. If you cook by Aga the final simmering should be done in the simmering oven. The stock from the joint can be used in soups and sauces. If it is too salty, mix it with water or another stock. A delicious meal to serve and very easy to prepare.

Black Cherry Sauce

100ml (4fl ozs) red Martini
50ml (2fl ozs) stock (preferably from the cooked ham or bacon joint)
2 tbls. redcurrant jelly
2 tbls. double cream
several pinches dried tarragon
1 tin pitted black cherries – drain from the juices

Put the Martini into a pan and boil to reduce a little. Whisk in the redcurrant jelly and when dissolved add all remaining ingredients, bring to a simmer before serving.

Lazy Cook tips – this sauce can be made in advance and reheated for serving. It can be served hot or cold. Store in a covered container in a fridge or cold larder, use within 4 days.

Layered Terrine of Pork

serves 10-12 slices
700ms (1½ lbs) fillet of pork
450gms (1 lb) streaky bacon – without rinds
1 bay leaf
1 small onion – skin and finely chop
175gms (6ozs) dark mushrooms – wipe and roughly chop
100gms (4ozs) lambs liver – cut into pieces
1 x 200gm pkt. bacon lardons
1 teas. Dijon mustard
100gms (4ozs) bread – break into pieces
½ teas. dried sage
freshly ground pepper
good squeeze fresh lemon juice
50gms (2ozs) pistachio nuts – shell and cut in half

Set oven at gas 6/450°F/220°C/Aga roasting oven. Lightly oil an 900gm (2 lb) loaf tin and place a bayleaf in the centre of the base, then line the base and sides with streaky bacon, stretched with a knife. Slice the fillet thickly. Soften the onion in a little boiling water with lid on pan then, using a slotted spoon, put into a food processor or liquidiser with the remaining ingredients. Process for a few seconds to form a sticky paste. Put a layer of fillet into the prepared tin and cover with half the paste then add another layer of fillet. Cover with the remaining paste and finally top with fillet and press down. Cover with foil and place in a meat tin, pour warm water to come half way up the tin (see Bain Marie). Put into the pre-set oven for 10mins. then reduce the temperature to gas 3/300vF/150°C/Aga simmering oven and continue to bake for 45mins. or until the terrine is firm to the touch. Remove from oven, cover the surface with a piece of card and press with a heavy weight, or tin. Remove from the meat tin and allow to become cold. To serve, remove the weight, card and foil, loosen the sides using a palette knife and turn the terrine on to a serving dish. Slice and serve as a starter or main course.

Lazy Cook tips – this is a very special terrine to make at Christmas or any party time. The flavours, colours and textures are good and look so attractive when sliced. Store wrapped in greaseproof then foil, in a fridge or cold larder. Use within 5 days.

The Christmas Turkey

I know of very few cooks who do not have nightmares about roasting the turkey. December 25th is the only day we have turkey and I have notes going back some 25 years on the different methods and oven temperatures I have followed. The luxury of my 4-oven Aga does not always guarantee success because the oven temperatures cannot be instantly adjusted. Even so I must be doing something right because the family returns each year for a repeat performance. Here are my tips on turkey roasting –

Think of the turkey as a large chicken, this will instantly alleviate all anxiety over the roasting. Begin by adding the approximate weight of a chosen stuffing to the weight of the turkey (without giblets), then work out the roasting time allowing 15mins. to each 450gms (1 lb). For example, for a turkey (including stuffing) weighing 6kgs (13½ lbs) the approximate roasting time should be 3hrs. 20mins. After roasting allow the turkey to rest for 30mins. before it is carved. As with all roasts, this allows the juices which have risen during roasting to fall and keep the turkey moist.

To prepare the turkey for roasting

Set oven at gas 6/450°F/220°C/Aga roasting oven.
Add the chosen stuffing to the turkey then place it on a trivet in a large roasting tin. Smear butter or oil over the skin and pour approx. 600ml (1 pt) boiling water into the pan. Put into the pre-set oven and roast for 30mins. Remove from the oven and cover completely with foil, return to oven and reduce the temperature to gas 4/400°F/200°C/Aga baking oven for the remainder of the roasting time. Remove from oven, remove the foil (taking care, hot steam may escape), and test by sticking a matchstick into the thickest part of the leg, if the juices run clear the turkey is cooked. If not, return to the oven and continue roasting and testing every 10mins. Loosen the foil while the turkey is resting, before carving.

Lazy Cook tips - the juices from the pan should be kept, pour them into a basin and when cold store them in a fridge or cold larder. They provide excellent stock for soups, sauces, bakes or casseroles. Remove any fat which will have set on the surface, before using. Use within 4 days or freeze.

A Vegetable Millefeuille garnished with a Wine and Herb Icing

serves 4-6
1 x 250gm. pkt. puff pastry
800gms (2 lbs) vegetables (a selection of your choice, all cut to a similar size)
1 teas. root ginger – grated
a good squeeze lemon juice
50gms (2ozs) seedless grapes – black or white
1 mandarin orange – break into segments
2 tbls. double cream
1 tbls. horseradish cream
75gms (3ozs) icing sugar
a little white wine
1 tbls. fresh parsley – chopped

Set oven at gas 7/475°F/240°C/Aga roasting oven.

Cut the pastry in half and roll each into a rectangle approx. 15cms x 20cms (6" x 8"). Put on a lightly oiled baking tray, prick lightly with a fork and bake in the pre-set oven for 10mins. or until the pastry has risen and is browning, turn over and bake for a further 10mins. or until brown. Remove from oven and keep warm while the filling is prepared. Add the selected vegetables to a small amount of boiling water and cook, with lid on pan, until they begin to soften. Stir in the grapes and orange segments before straining off the cooking liquid, then stir in the ginger. Mix the cream and horseradish together and stir into the vegetables, sandwich the pastry together with this. Make up a runny icing with the icing sugar and wine, stir in the parsley and spread this thinly on top. Slice to serve.

Lazy Cook tips – this is a delicious recipe to serve, hot or cold, especially if catering for vegetarians. It is full of good flavours, textures and colours.

Puddings

Boxing Day Pudding

cold Christmas pudding
brandy
425ml (¾pt) milk
1 teas. vanilla essence
3 large eggs

Set oven at gas 3/300°F/150°C/Aga simmering oven.
Slice the pudding thickly, put into a shallow ovenproof dish and sprinkle liberally with brandy. Warm the milk and vanilla essence, whisk the eggs and pour through a sieve into the warm milk.   Stir well before pouring over the pudding slices. Bake, uncovered, until set. Serve from the oven with single cream.

Christmas Pudding

The following is a very old Smith family recipe.   It might well be questioned whether making Christmas puddings comes under the heading of Lazy Cook, but I think of it as a part of the Christmas preparation not to be missed. I endeavour to make them when the family is around and we can each stir and wish.   I make an extra large one for our family Christmas Day lunch in the hope that there will be some remaining for a Boxing Day pudding.   I also make very small ones to give as presents, especially to friends living alone.

Makes 3 x 900gms (2lb) puddings
350gms (12ozs) raisins
350gms (12ozs) sultanas
350gms (12ozs) currants
225gms (8ozs) dark cane sugar
175gms (6ozs) mixed peel
175gms (6ozs) fresh breadcrumbs (brown or white)
350gms (12ozs) grated suet
175gms (6ozs) plain flour
1 teas. mixed spice
350gms (12ozs) grated cooking apple
50gms (2ozs) flaked almonds – browned
1 small carrot – grated
zest of 1 lemon
5 size 1 eggs – whisk together
100ml (4fl.oz) brandy
50gms (2ozs) butter
100gms (4ozs) whole almonds in their skins

Butter 3 basins spreading it thickly over the base and into this press whole almonds. Mix all the remaining ingredients together and pack into the basins. Cover with buttered greaseproof then foil (each pleated in the middle), and tie with string. Steam for 6-8hrs or until the puddings are dark and firm to the touch. Allow to cool before storing in a cool dry place. Reheat before serving.

Lazy Cook tips – one thing that deters people from making Christmas puddings is a kitchen full of steam. This can be avoided by steaming them in the oven. Stand the basins in a large roasting tin, pour in a kettle of boiling water and cover with foil. Put into the oven (gas 3/300°F/150°C/Aga simmering oven), for 6-8hrs. or until cooked. Add more boiling water as necessary although, unlike traditional steaming, it is no disaster if the pan runs dry. I put them in the oven overnight. Reheat in the oven or in a microwave before serving. Christmas puddings can be made as early as January, when cold remove them from the basins and wrap individually in a double layer of greaseproof then foil. Store in airtight tins in a cool dry place. They can also be made and frozen.

Dacquoise

serves 8-10
2 almond meringue plates (recipe on page 67)
100gms (4ozs) dried apricots
strip of lemon rind
50gms (2ozs) granulated sugar
juice of half a lemon
300ml (½pt) double cream
a little icing sugar
a little grated bitter chocolate for decoration

Put the apricots in a pan with the lemon rind, cover with cold water and simmer until they have softened.   Strain off the liquid and mix 50gms (2ozs) with the sugar and lemon juice, leave until cold. Discard remaining liquid.   Process or liquidise the apricots, lightly whip the cream and fold in to the apricots.   To assemble, sandwich the meringue plates with the apricot cream, sieve icing sugar on the top and scatter with grated chocolate.   Store in a fridge or cold larder for several hours to soften before serving.

Lazy Cook tips – for a more eye-catching presentation, reserve a little of the cream and about a tablespoon of the apricot puree before the juices have been added.   Pipe small circles of cream on top of the filled meringue (one per slice), and fill with apricot puree.   Sieve with icing sugar and grated chocolate as directed in the recipe.   Rather than grating chocolate, I find it easier to cut off shavings using a sharp knife, it is easily done especially if the chocolate is really cold.   I cannot take credit for this recipe although I have simplified the method.   It was given me by Ra, an aunt-in-law, an excellent cook and hostess who taught me so much.

Almond Meringue Plates

makes 2 x 25cms (10")
4 x size 1 egg whites
225gms (8ozs) caster sugar
pinch cream of tartare
75gms (3ozs) sliced almonds – brown slightly and finely chop

Set oven at gas 2/200°F/100°C/Aga simmering oven.
Cover 2 baking trays with household parchment or bake-o-glide. Whisk the egg whites until they are stiff and dry (of a cottonwool texture). Fold in the sugar, cream of tartare and almonds then spread the mixture equally on to the prepared baking trays in rounds approx. 25cms (10") in diameter. Place in the pre-set oven to dry (this can take between 2 and 4 hours). Take from oven and remove from paper. When cold store in airtight polythene or freezer bags until needed.

Lazy Cook tips – these meringue plates will remain crisp for 2 months.

Dried Fruit Compote

Take a selection of dried fruit (prunes, apricots, pears, peaches etc), about 225gms (8ozs) in weight. Cover with fresh orange juice (from a carton). Add a cinnamon stick and bring to a simmer. Put lid on pan and simmer until the fruit has softened. Remove the cinnamon stick before serving the fruit hot, warm or cold. Cook in advance and store, covered, in a fridge or cold larder.

Lazy Cook tips – if you cook by Aga the simmering should be done in the simmering oven. It is possible to buy dried fruit pre-soaked but if it is not, soak it in the orange juice for a few hours before cooking. Sweeten with clear honey if the flavour is too tart for your palate. A selection of dried fruits is an excellent ingredient to have in store especially during the autumn and winter months when seasonal fruits are past their best.

Fruit Pizza

serves 6-8
1 pizza base (wholemeal if possible)
2-3tbls. orange marmalade
225gms (8ozs) mixed dried fruit
1 large bramley apple
a few glacé cherries – cut in half
a few pinches cinnamon powder
1 tbls. demerera sugar

Set oven at gas 6/450°F/220°C/Aga roasting oven.
Place the pizza base on a large baking tray, spread it with marmalade and top with dried fruit. Peel and quarter the apple, remove and discard core, cut the quarters into slices and cover the dried fruit with these and press down. Scatter with a few halves of glacé cherries, sprinkle with cinnamon then demerera sugar. Bake for 20-30mins. or until the apples have softened. Slice to serve hot, warm or cold, with ice cream or single or whipped cream.

Lazy Cook tips – this is a somewhat different way of using a pizza base, very quick to prepare and very tasty. Pizza bases are available in delicatessens and supermarkets.

Iced Christmas Pudding

serves 6-8
50gms (2 ozs) raisins
25gms (1 oz) sultanas
25gms (1 oz) currants
3 tbls. brandy
150ml (¼pt) milk
100gms (4ozs) marshmallows
1 teas. cocoa powder
1 teas. instant coffee powder
50gms (2ozs) glacé cherries
50gms (2ozs) walnuts – chopped
300ml (½pt) double cream
for decoration – 150ml (¼pt) double cream
                    a few glacé cherries
                    angelica

Mix the dried fruit together and soak in the brandy for at least 30mins. Put the milk, marshmallows, cocoa and coffee into a saucepan and heat gently until the marshmallows have melted. Allow to cool before stirring in the dried fruit, brandy, cherries and nuts. Put into a 1 ltr (2pt) basin and freeze until it begins to thicken. Whip the cream and fold into the freezing mixture, repack into the basin and freeze until you wish to serve it. To serve, remove from the freezer and when it begins to soften turn it on to a serving dish.. Put into a fridge or cold larder for 2hrs. to allow it to thaw but retain its shape. To decorate, lightly whip 150ml (¼pt) double cream and pour it on top of the pudding allowing it to run down the sides and top with cherries, angelica and nuts.

Lazy Cook tips – stick a metal skewer into the centre to test whether it is completely thawed. A delicious pudding and too good to restrict to serving only at Christmas. It can be made and frozen well in advance of serving.

Mincemeat and Ginger Thins

to make 4
12 ginger thins (biscuits)
mincemeat (recipe on page 121)
apple purée (recipe on page 121)
150ml (¼ pt) double cream
for decoration – holly leaves and berries (recipe on page 117)

To assemble, cover a ginger thin with mincemeat, top with a second ginger thin and cover this with apple purée, top with a third ginger thin. Whip the cream and drop a spoon of this on to the top ginger thin. Leave in a fridge or cold larder, uncovered, for about an hour before serving. To serve, press holly leaves and berries into the cream and sieve with a little icing sugar

Lazy Cook tips – these can be made using bought mincemeat and apple purée. Ginger Thins are very thin ginger biscuits with a decorative edge, available at most shops and supermarkets. For an alternative decoration, top with crystalised ginger, chocolate squares (recipe on page 37), or grated chocolate, or simply sprinkle with a good pinch of ground ginger.

Mincemeat Tart with Apple and Cinnamon

serves 6-8
1 ready baked pastry case
1 jar mincemeat
1 bramley apple
ground cinnamon

Set oven at gas 4/400°F/200°C/Aga baking oven.
Fill the pastry case to just below the top with mincemeat. Peel the apple, cut into quarters and remove the core. Cut each quarter into slices and arrange these, slightly overlapping, on top of the mincemeat. Sprinkle with ground cinnamon and bake until the apple has softened. Serve hot, warm or cold with cream or ice cream.

Lazy Cook tips – make this pudding quickly using a ready-baked flan case available from supermarkets and delicatessens. The apple and cinnamon completes the blend of flavours and so reminiscent of Christmas. Best made with home-made mincemeat (recipe on page 121), or one of the luxury varieties from a delicatessen or supermarket.

Mincemeat Tart with a Macaroon Topping

serves 6-8
1 ready baked pastry case
mincemeat
2 egg whites
225gms (8ozs) caster sugar
100gms (4ozs) ground almonds
12gms (½ oz) plain flour
few spots vanilla essence
split almonds for decoration

Set oven at gas 4/400°F/200°C/Aga baking oven.
Spread the mincemeat to come almost to the top of the pastry case. Whisk the whites until stiff and dry. Mix the sugar, ground almonds and sifted flour together and fold into the whites with the vanilla essence. Spread this to cover the mincemeat and touch the sides of the pastry case. Spike with split almonds and bake in the pre-set oven for 15-20mins. Serve hot, warm or cold

Lazy Cook tips – reduce the oven temperature slightly after 10mins. if the meringue is becoming too brown. A delicious recipe though quite rich. More advice on meringue making on page 119.

Tipsy Pudding

serves 6-8
3 desst. orange marmalade
6 desst. sweet sherry
6 desst. brandy
100gms (4ozs) crystalised pineapple pieces
50gms (2ozs) crystalised ginger pieces
100gms (4ozs) glacé cherries of mixed colours
ginger cake (recipe on page 113)
For decoration – 300ml (½pt) double cream
                        2 tbls. ginger wine

Put the marmalade, sherry and brandy into a pan and heat until the marmalade has dissolved.   Add the pineapple, ginger and cherries (reserving a few of each for decoration).   Mix in enough ginger cake, broken into pieces, to absorb the liquid and make a sticky mixture.   Pack into a basin, cover with a saucer and a weight and leave in a fridge or cold larder for 24hrs.   To serve, loosen the sides using a palette knife and turn the cake on to a serving dish.   Whip the cream and ginger wine together and spread all over the cake.   Spike with the reserved fruits and ginger.

Lazy Cook tips – quite a rich pudding, serve small slices!   Very easy to make and very delicious flavours.   Ready made ginger cake can be used.

Traditional Sherry Trifle

serves 8-10
850ml (1½pts) full cream milk
2 heaped desst. custard powder
1 desst. sugar
few drops vanilla essence
1 pkt. trifle sponges
strawberry jam
300ml (½pt) sweet sherry
1 x 410gm tin strawberries
300ml (½pt) double cream
flaked almonds – lightly browned
glacé cherries

Mix the custard powder to a runny paste with a little of the milk. Warm the remaining milk before adding the custard powder mixture and the sugar, stir until it boils. Stir in the vanilla essence, remove from heat and leave to cool a little. Split the trifle sponges and spread each with a little strawberry jam. Place in a large deep trifle dish, add the sherry and mash with a fork. Top with strawberries (strain off the juice), then cover with the custard and leave to set. To serve, spread the top with lightly whipped cream and scatter with flaked almonds and glacé cherry halves.

Lazy Cook tips – a traditional sherry trifle is always a popular pudding to serve. This is a recipe my Mother would have used when eggs were too scarce to use in puddings. Take care not to make the custard too thick, it will thicken more as it sets. Because of the sweetness of the ingredients I add very little sugar to the custard. Make this trifle a day before it is to be served and store, covered, in a fridge or cold larder. Add the cream and decoration before serving.

Winter Fresh Fruit Salad

Towards the end of winter a new variety of fresh fruits appear in the supermarkets, imports from warmer climates ahead of our own seasonal summer fruits. At such times I find it refreshing to use these to make a fresh fruit salad.

serves 4
1 mango – peel and slice
1 punnet of strawberries – wash and cut in half
225gms (8ozs) seedless grapes (red or white)
1 teas. sugar
1 teas. orange flower water
2 tbls. Cointreau

Mix all the fruit in a serving dish. Dissolve the sugar in a little hot water and flavour with orange flower water and Cointreau. Pour over the fruit and allow to become cold before serving.

Recommended Menus

Christmas Eve

I am full of admiration for people who manage to entertain on Christmas Eve. I find there are so many last-minute things to be done, but if I were ever able to contemplate this, the following is a menu I might offer, inviting friends to drop in at any time during the evening.

page

Ginger Wine

∘ ∘ O ∘ ∘

Cocktail Blinis	50
Baked Avocado with Goats Cheese	49
Savoury Rice	124

∘ ∘ O ∘ ∘

Mincemeat Tart with Apple and Cinmamon, served with Whisky Flavoured Cream	70

∘ ∘ O ∘ ∘

Coffee

Christmas Day Lunch

My book "Enter the New Millennium with Lazy Cook Mo Smith" features recipes for a traditional Christmas Day including lunch, tea and supper menus, but the above is a recommended alternative lunch menu if you wish to break with tradition, or if you are few in number.

Boxing Day
a meal following a walk

"Fridge-ends" Lunch Party

Local friends often join us for a very impromptu lunch sometime between Christmas and the New Year. We all crowd round one table and enjoy a very relaxed, noisy lunch which goes on well into the afternoon – one of my favourite ways of entertaining. The following is an example of the menu I might serve, always depending on what left-overs are available.

page

Platter of Cold Meats
Pork Terrine   55

o o O o o

Jacket Potatoes   130
Salad of Chopped Celery, Carrot   132
and Spring Onions
Watercress and Salad Leaves
Pickles and Chutneys
Assorted Bread and Rolls

o o O o o

Fruit Pizza and Cream   68
Dried Fruit Compote   67

o o O o o

Cheese and Biscuits

o o O o o

Coffee

Teenage Party
fork buffet

New Year's Eve Dinner Party

January to Easter

Many people dislike the beginning of a new year.   Following the excitement of Christmas it seems dull and flat.   The days are cold and the evenings dark and long and to some it is quite a depesssing time of year.

In recent years I have come to really look forward to the months of January and February.   There is no more panic buying of food or presents and endless shopping lists to be made.   No Christmas cards to write, decorations to put up, lights to fix .   It is a time to draw breath, a time to relax in front of a video or catch up on some reading.   A time to shed those extra pounds put on during the Christmas festivities by exercising at the gym or taking a regular walk.   A time to reflect, and a time, perhaps, to make a batch of marmalade before Burns Night, Valentine's Day, Shrove Tuesday and Easter are upon us.

Index of Recipes

Starters and Light Meals

Main Courses

Puddings

Starters and Light Meals

Burnt Red Pepper Soup

serves 4
olive oil
2 red peppers
1 red onion – skin and chop
850ml (1½pts) stock
freshly ground pepper
good pinch herbes de Provence
2 tbls. single cream

Quarter the peppers, discard the stalk, inside pips and fleshy bits.   Brush the skin with oil and place in a lightly oiled ovenproof dish and brown under a hot grill or in a hot oven (gas 6/450°F/220°C/Aga roasting oven) until the skins begin to burn.   Soften the prepared onion in a large pan in a little boiling water, with lid on pan.   Process or liquidise the peppers with the onion, return to the pan, add the stock and season with pepper and herbes.   Simmer for 10-15mins. with lid on pan.   Add the cream, bring back to a simmer before serving.

Lazy Cook tips – if you cook by Aga the simmering process should be done in the simmering oven.   A very quick soup rich in colour and flavour. Can be made in advance and stored, covered, in a fridge or cold larder.

Cheesie Eggs

serves 4-6
6 eggs – medium/hard boiled
25gms (1oz) butter
25gms (1oz) plain flour
600ml (1pt) milk
100gms (4ozs) Gruyere cheese – grated
2 tbls. single cream
fresh chives – snip with scissors
freshly ground white pepper

Set oven at gas 6/450°F/220°C/Aga roasting oven.
Shell and slice the eggs and arrange over the base of a shallow ovenproof dish. Melt the butter in a pan, stir in the flour and cook over a gentle heat until it blends into a smooth paste. Add the milk and continue stirring until the sauce boils, boil until it thickens. Remove from heat, stir in the cheese, cream, chives and pepper and pour over the eggs. Bake in the pre-set oven (or under a grill) until it is hot and bubbly before serving.

Lazy Cook tips – should the sauce become lumpy, remove it from the heat and whisk until smooth before continuing to cook. This recipe can be prepared in individual ramekins. Serve as a starter or as a light meal. Prepare in advance and store, covered, in a fridge or cold larder.

Cheese Soufflé

I believe hot soufflés are amongst the most neglected of savoury dishes - there is a myth about them which implies they can only be produced by top chefs in expensive restaurants, this is not so, they are really very simple to prepare and bake. Read through my Lazy Cook tips and you will find the following, and other soufflé recipes, so easy to cook and your guests will love them.

serves 4-6
25gms (1oz) butter
12gms (½oz) plain flour
150ml (¼pt) milk
3 egg yolks
a few pinches of mustard powder
a few pinches of cayenne pepper
4 egg whites
50gms (2ozs) mature Stilton – grated
50gms (2ozs) Gruyere – grated
a little grated Parmesan for a final garnish

Set oven at gas 4/400°F/200°C/Aga baking oven.

Butter well the base and sides of one large (size 2) porcelain soufflé dish. Tie a piece of buttered greaseproof round the outside to project about 5cms (2") above the rim and secure the ends with a paperclip. Stand the prepared dish on a baking tray. Melt the butter in a pan large enough to take all the ingredients. Remove it from the heat before the butter becomes too hot and stir in the flour until a smooth consistency, (this is called a roux). Stir in the milk. Return to a gentle heat and stir until it thickens, remove from heat and allow to cool just a little before beating in the egg yolks and several good pinches each of mustard powder and cayenne pepper. Whisk the egg whites until they peak and fold in one tablespoon, and the cheeses, into the roux. Carefully fold in the remaining egg white and pour into the prepared dish. Put immediately into the pre-set oven and bake for 20-30mins. or until risen and set. Serve straight from the oven with the paper removed and grated parmesan scattered on top.

Lazy Cook tips – the secrets of success are to have all the ingredients to hand, the cheeses grated, the oven up to temperature and the dish prepared before beginning to make the soufflé. I recommend the butter is melted but not hot before the flour is added, this will ensure a smooth paste (roux). Soufflés rise from below and if you cook by Aga place it on the floor of the baking oven. I like soufflés crisp on the outside and spongy in the middle – test by piercing the cente with a metal skewer, preferably warm. Bring the guests to the table a few minutes before the soufflé is baked and carry it to the table on a hot serving plate. Test on the family so that you know exactly how long it will take to bake!

Mushroom Crêpe with Coriander

makes 4
175gms (6ozs) mushrooms – wipe and slice
150ml (¼pt) milk
25gms (1oz) butter
1 teas. mushroom ketchup
freshly ground pepper
1 desst. plain flour
a little extra milk
a handful of fresh coriander
4 crêpe (recipe on page 98)

Heat the milk and butter in a pan, add the prepared mushrooms, put lid on pan and simmer for a minute or two until the mushrooms begin to soften. Remove from heat and season with mushroom ketchup and pepper. Add the flour to a little cold milk and stir to a smooth paste. Stir into the mushroom mixture, and gently bring to a boil, boil until the sauce thickens, stirring continuously. Divide the mixture between the crêpe and add a little coriander before folding over to make a crescent shape. Place on a lightly oiled baking tray and heat under a hot grill, in a microwave, or hot oven (gas 6/450°F/220°C/Aga roasting oven). Serve as a starter or main course.

Lazy Cook tips – these are very good to serve as a starter or a light meal, especially if catering for vegetarians. Thin the sauce down with a little single cream if it is too thick. Make in advance and store, covered, in a fridge or cold larder.

Pea and Ham Soup

serves 4
1 large onion – skin and chop
1 x 200gm pkt. bacon lardons
850ml (1½pts) stock
2 tbls. plain flour
little milk
1 x 200gm tin petits pois
mint (fresh or dried)
2fl.oz single cream

Smear the base of the pan with oil and when hot add the prepared onion and the lardons and cook, with lid on pan, over a gentle heat. Mix the flour to a smooth paste with a little cold milk and add this, and the stock, to the pan. Bring to a boil and boil for about a minute, stirring continuously. Add the petits pois and mint and season with freshly ground white pepper. Put lid on pan and simmer for 5-10mins. Stir in the cream, bring back to a simmer and serve.

Lazy Cook tips – I recommend a mixture of ham and chicken stock is used in this recipe (stock-making recipes on page 125). It is quick to make and a good soup to serve hot in winter or cold in summer, when fresh garden mint is available.

Pepper Cups filled with an Anchovy Paste and served with a Last-Minute Sauce

serves 4
2 peppers
1 tbls. oil
25gms (1oz) brown breadcrumbs
25gms (1oz) cooked ham or bacon
6 anchovy fillets
4 pitted black olives
2 sundried tomatoes
1 teas. pesto
1 teas. olive oil
freshly ground pepper
1 tbls. fresh parsley – chopped
1 tomato
a few shavings of butter

Set oven at gas 6/450°F/220°C/Aga roasting oven.
Cut the peppers in half so that each half has some of the green stem. Remove seeds and fleshy bits.   Place the peppers, cut side down in a lightly oiled ovenproof dish, brush with oil and bake in the pre-set oven until the skins begin to soften and brown (15-20mins).   Reserving a little of the parsley, the tomato and the butter, put all the remaining ingredients into a food processor or liquidiser and process to a sticky paste.   Turn the browned pepper halves over and fill each with the paste, top with a slice of tomato, a dot of butter and a sprinkling of fresh parsley and return to the oven for 5-10mins. to soften the tomato.   Serve with a little salad garnish and Last-Minute Sauce (recipe on page 87).

Lazy Cook tips – I recommend anchovy fillets preserved in oil and now available from delicatessen counters.   If catering for a lot of people I choose peppers of assorted colours, they look really good presented on a large serving platter.   A recipe with excellent flavours.

Last-Minute Sauce - *to serve with Roast Peppers*

Put 5ozs hot water (or vegetable stock), into the dish in which the peppers have been baked, whisk in a couple of shakes of tomato ketchup, bring to a boil and serve.

Main Courses

Chicken with Apricots and Almonds

serves 6-8
450gms (1 lb) cooked chicken – break into mouthsized pieces
250gms (8ozs) mushrooms – wipe and slice
100gms (4ozs) dried apricots – cut into strips
a good sprinkling dried tarragon
1 x 205gm tin Campbells condensed mushroom soup
150ml (¼pt) white wine
150ml (¼pt) single cream
50gms (2ozs) flaked almonds – browned

Set oven at gas 6/450°F/220°C/Aga roasting oven.
Layer the chicken, mushrooms and apricots into a shallow ovenproof dish and add the tarragon. Put the soup, wine and cream into a pan and stir until boiling then pour it over the chicken ingredients. Scatter flaked almonds on top and bake, uncovered, in the pre-set oven for 20-30mins. or until hot and bubbling.

Lazy Cook tips - prepare it in advance and store, covered, in a fridge or cold larder and reheat to serve. I serve boiled rice and mixed vegetables with this recipe. It is an excellent recipe if catering for lots of people, I have made it in vast quantities to serve at fund-raising suppers, assembled in huge casseroles and preserving pans. For such occasions use whole cooked chickens. This recipe can also be prepared using cooked turkey.

Chicken Rolls with Curly Cabbage

makes 8 rolls
8 boned chicken thighs
100gms (4ozs) chicken liver paté
8 rashers streaky bacon – unsmoked
300ml (½pt) white wine
1 curly cabbage – wash and slice

Set oven at gas 6/450°F/220°C/Aga roasting oven.
Spread each thigh with paté and roll up then roll in a bacon rasher.   Put
into a shallow ovenproof dish, add the wine and bake, uncovered, for
20mins.   Cook the cabbage in a little boiling water until tender, drain off
the liquid and keep.   Dry the cabbage by returning it to the pan and
stirring it over a gentle heat, then place it down the centre of a hot serving
dish.   Put the cooked chicken thighs on top.   Add a little of the reserved
cabbage water to the pan juices and boil to reduce a little.   Spoon some
over the cooked chicken and serve the remainder separately.

*Lazy Cook tips – boned chicken thighs are available in most supermarkets,
they have an excellent flavour and this is a tasty and colourful way to
serve them.   A ready-made paté is quickest to use, or the following recipe
can be made.*

Chicken Liver Paté

50gms (2ozs) butter
1 shallot – skin and finely chop
225gms (8ozs) chicken livers
2 tbls. brandy
1 dried bayleaf
2 good pinches herbes de Provence
freshly ground white pepper
extra butter for sealing

Soften the shallot in half the butter.   Add the remaining butter and when melted add the chicken livers and cook for approximately 2 mins. turning them halfway through cooking, remove from pan.   Scrape any bits from the base of the pan, add the brandy and boil for a few seconds, remove from heat and allow to cool slightly before putting into a food processor or liquidiser with the cooked livers and onion.   Process until smooth.   Pack into a pot.   Melt approx. 50gms (2ozs) butter and pour over the paté to form a seal and when set store in a fridge.   Allow to come back to room temperature before serving.   Use within 7 days.

Lazy Cook tips – this is an excellent paté to serve with toast as a quick starter.

Crown of Lamb served with a Red Wine and Pesto Sauce

This is another recipe I have resurrected from my very early days of cooking.   Although it looks so majestic as the title suggests, it is one of the easiest of dinner party recipes.   I served this to friends before leaving London to be married.   It was a memorable and noisy party, not least the entry of the Crown of Lamb.

serves 6
1 crown of lamb – prepared by a butcher
1 bunch watercress
cutlet frills (one for each cutlet)
300ml (½pt) red wine
1 tbls. pesto
1 tbls. redcurrant jelly

Set the oven at gas 6/450°F/220°C/Aga roasting oven.
Weigh the crown and allow 15mins. per 450gms(1 lb) to serve pink, or 20mins. per 450gms (1 lb) to serve well done.   Stand the crown on a trivet in a meat tin and add about 300ml (½pt) hot water.   Put in the pre-set oven and roast for 10mins. then reduce the oven temperature to gas 4/400°F/200°C/Aga baking oven for the remainder of the roasting time. Remove from the oven, put on a hot serving dish and keep warm.   Spoon any excess fat from the pan juices before adding the wine and boil for a few minutes to reduce.   Whisk in the pesto and redcurrent jelly and bring to a simmer.   To serve, place a cutlet frill on each cutlet and fill the centre cavity with fresh watercress.   Serve the sauce separately.

Lazy Cook tips – I recommend 2 cutlets per person and you may find 2 crowns are needed.

Devilled Lamb

serves 4
4 fillets of lamb
2fl.ozs double cream
2fl.ozs sour cream
2 tbls. Worcestershire sauce
1 tbls. sundried tomato purée
1 teas. anchovy essence
½ teas dried mint
2fl.ozs wine - red or white
freshly ground pepper

Trim any excess fat from the fillets before cutting them into mouthsized pieces.   Mix all the remaining ingredients together, pour on to the lamb, stir well then leave to marinade for 2-3hrs.   To cook, bring the marinaded ingredients to a simmer over a gentle heat.   Put lid on pan and simmer for 45mins to 1 hr. or until the meat is tender.   Serve hot or cold.

Lazy Cook tips – for a more concentrated flavour allow the meat to marinade overnight.   If cooking by Aga the simmering process should be done in the simmering oven.

Family Cheese Pie

serves 6-8
225gms (8ozs) plain white (or wholemeal) flour
100gms (4ozs) lard
2-3 fl.ozs cold water
1 large onion – skin and chop
1 tbls. cooking oil
1 x 100gm tin chopped tomatoes
pinch sugar
good sprinkling of herbs – fresh or dried
175gms (6ozs) strong Cheddar cheese – grated
150ml (¼pt) warmed milk
3 large eggs
freshly ground white pepper
several pinches English mustard powder

Set oven at gas 6/450°F/220°C/Aga roasting oven.
Make a pastry by putting the flour and fat into a food processor, process for a few seconds before pouring in water until a ball of pastry is formed, switch off. Lightly oil a deep pie dish, roll out the pastry large enough to line the base and sides, prick the base with a fork and bake in the pre-set oven for 15-20mins. Remove from oven and reduce the temperature to gas 4/400°F/200°C/Aga baking oven. Heat the oil in a pan, add the prepared onion and cook until it begins to soften and spread over the base of the cooked pastry. Top with tomatoes seasoned with sugar and herbs, then with grated cheese. Whisk the eggs and stir into the warmed milk with the pepper and mustard powder. Pour through a sieve on to the cheese and bake for 1 hr. or until set and brown on top. Serve straight from the oven with boiled rice.

Lazy Cook tips – this is an excellent pie and so quick to prepare. It does not matter how unevenly the pastry is rolled or patched when lining the dish. I have adapted this recipe from a similar pie we as a family were served many years ago when we visited friend Annie. I baked it many times when the children were at home and it became a family favourite, affectionately known as A.C.P.(Annie's Cheese Pie). It's a good recipe for using up any odd ends of cheese.

Fish Chowder

serves 4-6
1 large onion – skin and chop
100gms (4ozs) unsmoked bacon – cut into pieces
2 sticks celery – slice
100gms (4ozs) mushrooms – wipe and slice
900gms (2lbs) potatoes – peel and cut into mouthsized pieces
1 x 400gm tin sweetcorn – drain off juices
900gms (2lbs) white fish– cut into mouthsized pieces
2 tbls. flour seasoned with freshly ground white pepper
150ml (¼pt) thick single cream
2 teas. Dijon mustard
freshly chopped parsley – lots

Soften the onion, bacon, celery and mushrooms in a little boiling water with lid on pan.   Add the potatoes and sufficient cold water to cover. Bring to a simmer and simmer, with lid on pan, until the potatoes are almost cooked before adding the sweetcorn.   Coat the fish pieces in the seasoned flour and place on top of the pan ingredients.   Bring back to a simmer and continue simmering with lid on pan for 10mins. or until the fish has cooked.   Stir in the cream, mustard and parsley and bring back to a simmer before serving with warm rolls or chunks of bread.

Lazy Cook tips – cod cheeks are excellent for this recipe.   If you cook by Aga the simmering process should be done in the simmering oven.   Serve this recipe for lunch or supper.

Risotto

serves 4-6
1 large onion – skin and chop
1 tbls. cooking oil
225gms (8ozs) cooked brown rice (recipe on page 123)
350gms (12ozs) cooked chicken, ham or liver
175gms (6ozs) mushrooms – wipe and slice
4 celery stalks – slice
50gms (2ozs) browned cashew nuts
50gms (2ozs) dried apricots – slice
several good pinches mixed dried herbs
freshly ground white pepper
150ml (¼pt) coconut milk, or stock
sliced almonds – browned

Heat the oil in a large pan, add the onion and cook until beginning to soften, with lid on pan.   Add all the remaining ingredients and stir over a gentle heat until hot throughout, serve.

Lazy Cook tips – this recipe is excellent for using up any cooked ends of meat, poultry, sausages or fish.   In summer I serve it cold adding fresh herbs and summer fruits, (including wild strawberries freshly picked from the garden), cherries or small seedless grapes.   A little single cream or butter can be stirred in at the end of cooking.

Skate Wings with a Rhubarb Sauce

serves 4
4 skate wings
butter
bunch watercress
rhubarb sauce (recipe on page 94)

Heat a good knob of butter in a large frying pan.   Wipe the skate with kitchen roll and cook in the butter for 2-3mins on each side.   Serve on individual or one large dish with a garnish of watercress and serve the sauce separately.

Rhubarb Sauce

several sticks young rhubarb
clear honey
orange flower water

Wash and top and tail the rhubarb before cutting into slices approx. 5mm (½") thickness.   Soften in a little boiling water with lid on pan.   Sweeten with honey and flavour with a few dashes of orange flower water.   Serve hot or cold.

Lazy Cook tips – avoid adding too much honey especially when serving with savoury recipes.

Spicy Pork with Beansprouts and Pasta

serves 4
1 pork fillet
1 tbls. flour seasoned with a little freshly ground pepper
1 tbls. oil
1 teas. paprika
1 teas. tomato purée
garlic – optional
1 medium sized onion – skin and chop
150ml (¼pt) wine (red or white)
1 tbls. single cream
1 x 410gm tin beansprouts
cooked pasta

Slice the fillet into mouthsized pieces and coat each piece lightly in seasoned flour.   Heat the oil, add the fillet pieces and brown in the hot oil, remove from pan.   To the pan juices add the paprika, tomato purée and approx. 1fl.oz water.   Stir well then add the prepared onion, place lid on pan, and cook until the onion begins to soften.   Return the fillet pieces and the wine to the pan, and simmer, with lid on pan, for 10-15mins. (or until the fillet has cooked).   Stir in the cream and beansprouts and bring back to a simmer before serving on a bed of cooked pasta.   Garnish with chopped parsley or coriander

Lazy Cook tips – wet ingredients will not seal or brown quickly.   Dry the fillet on kitchen roll before lightly coating in the seasoned flour.   A very quick and tasty recipe.

Veal and Bacon Parcels with a Sundried Tomato Sauce

makes 8
1 pkt (340gms) minced or ground veal
1 desst. olive oil
1 teas Dijon mustard
1 teas. dried sage
1 egg yolk
1-2 tbls. fresh brown or white breadcrumbs (recipe on page 111)
freshly ground white pepper
16 slices rindless back bacon – unsmoked
2 teas. sundried tomato purée
a little stock
pinch sugar
freshly ground white pepper

Set oven at gas 6/450°F/220°C/Aga roasting oven.

Cook the veal in a little hot oil breaking it down with a fork. Stir in the mustard and sage, remove from heat and allow to cool a little before stirring in the egg yolk and enough breadcrumbs to make a sticky consistency. Using 2 slices of bacon for each parcel, arrange these like a cross and pile the paste at the point where the slices cross. Make into a parcel by tightly covering the paste with the ends of bacon, finishing with a lean end. Put the parcels back into the pan in which the veal was cooked, loose ends down. Brush each with oil and sprinkle with dried sage. Bake in the pre-set oven for 10-15mins. (or until the bacon has cooked). Remove from oven and put on to a hot serving dish and keep warm. Make the sauce by skimming any excess fat from the pan then whisk into the pan juices 2 teas. sundried tomato purée and a good pinch sugar. Add 150ml (¼pt) stock and a little freshly ground white pepper and simmer for a few minutes. Pour a little round the parcels and serve the remainder separately.

Lazy Cook tips – these parcels are remarkably quick to make and look so pretty when cooked. They are also quite filling, allow one per person plus a few spares. I serve them hot with leeks and rice. I also serve them cold as follows – cut them into slices and arrange 2 or 3 on individual serving plates, garnish with pickled cucumbers cut into fan shapes, a small bunch of red seedless grapes and a few salad leaves. Serve the sauce separately.

Puddings

Apple Gateau

serves 6-8
1 pkt. (24) sponge fingers or boudoir biscuits
450gms (1 lb) apple purée (recipe on page 121)
300ml (½pt) double cream
grated bitter chocolate or chocolate squares (recipe on page 37)

Line the base and ends of a 900gm (2lb) loaf tin with greaseproof paper or foil.   Fill with layers of sponge fingers sandwiched with apple purée beginning and ending with sponge fingers.   Cover with a piece of card wrapped in foil and press with a light weight, leave overnight in a fridge or cold larder.   To serve, remove the weight and card and loosen the sides with a palette knife, turn on to a servingdish.   Cover with whipped cream and scatter with grated chocolate or press chocolate squares into the sides and ends and spiked into the top.   Slice to serve.

Lazy Cook tips – a light and delicious pudding which can be made two or three days in advance and stored in a fridge or cold larder, add the cream before serving.

Crêpe and Pancakes

The Batter

300ml (½pt) milk
100gms (4ozs) plain flour
2 large eggs
2 tbls. sunflower oil
2 tbls. cold water
butter for cooking

Put the milk into a food processor, add the flour, eggs and oil and process for a few seconds until smooth. Pour into a jug, cover and put in a fridge or cold larder for 30mins. to 1 hour   Take from the fridge and whisk in 2tbls. cold water before making into crêpe or pancakes.

Crêpe

to make
Heat a 15cm (6") pan, smear the base with butter and pour in just enough batter to lightly coat the base (approx. 2tbls).   When set turn it over using a wooden spatula and cook for a few seconds more before turning on to a wire tray.   Use hot or cold with savoury or sweet fillings.

Lazy Cook tips – a crêpe pan should have a heavy base which must be really hot before the batter is added otherwise you will end up with a soggy mess.   A 300ml (½pt) batter mixture makes approx. 36 crêpe. Store or freeze them in stacks of 10 or 12 interleaving each crêpe with a piece of greaseproof.   Wrap in clingfilm and use within 5 days or put into freezer bags and freeze.   Use directly from the freezer easing between the layers with a palatte knife.   It will be obvious from the recipes I give in this book that crêpe are a most useful ingredient to have in store.   Ready-made crêpe can be bought in specialist delicatessens and supermarkets.

Pancakes

to make
Heat a 20cm (8") pan, smear the base with butter and pour in batter to cover.   Allow to set before turning over using a wooden spatula (or if you are brave toss it)!   Cook for a few seconds more before removing from pan and serving.

Lazy Cook tips – I think the only way to serve pancakes on Shrove Tuesday or any other day, is straight from the pan.   Turn the cooked pancake on to a hot plate, pour lemon juice over, add a little caster sugar, roll and eat.

Banana and Ginger Crêpe in a Brandy Cream Sauce

to make 8
150ml (¼pt) brandy
150ml (¼pt) ginger wine
50gms (2ozs) preserved ginger – slice
2 bananas – peel and slice
300ml (½pt) single cream
8 crêpe (recipe on page 98)

Put the brandy and ginger wine into a large shallow pan and boil to reduce a little.   Stir in the ginger, banana and cream, and bring to a simmer, remove from heat.   Move the ginger and banana to one side of the pan. Add the crêpe (one at a time), and fill with ginger and banana and a little sauce.   Fold over into a crescent shape and remove to a shallow ovenproof dish.   Pour the remaining sauce on top, cover with foil and heat in a low oven before serving (gas 3/300°F/150°C/Aga simmering oven).

Lazy Cook tips – a fish slice or wooden spatula will help you remove the filled crêpe from the pan.   Place them slightly overlapping in the ovenproof dish.   They can be prepared in advance.   Put them to warm in the simmering oven at the beginning of the meal and they will be just right to serve at pudding time.

Brandysnap Cups filled with Banana Slices and Spiced Cream, decorated with Bitter Chocolate Lace

serves 8
8 brandysnap cups
4 large bananas
300ml (½pt) double cream
1 tbls. sherry
1 teas. cocoa powder
¼ teas. mixed spice
¼ teas. cinnamon powder
a grating of nutmeg
chocolate lace (recipe on page 37)

Fill each cup with banana slices. Add the sherry, cocoa, spices and nutmeg to the cream and whip. Drop from a tablespoon on to the banana slices and spike with a piece of chocolate lace.

Lazy Cook tips – packets of ready-made brandysnap cups can be purchased in delicatessens and supermarkets. Scatter grated chocolate on the cream if you do not have any chocolate lace. Do not make too far in advance of serving.

Coffee Cracknell Meringue Ring

serves 6
3 egg whites
175gms (6ozs) caster sugar
1 teas. coffee granules
1 tbls. hot water
300ml (½pt) double cream
2 Crunchie bars (standard size)

Using the egg whites and caster sugar make 2 meringue rings following the recipe on page 120. To assemble, dissolve the coffee granules in hot water and add to the cream before whipping to a spreading consistency. Slice or chop the Crunchie bars into small pieces and stir all but a tablespoon into the cream, sandwich the meringue rings together with half of this and spread the remainder on top. Scatter with the reserved Crunchie and leave in a fridge or cold larder for an hour or more before serving.

Lazy Cook tips – a very quick and delicious pudding to make. Ready made meringue shapes can be used.

Hot Orange Pudding

serves 4
4 tbls. orange marmalade
2 oranges
1 pkt ready rolled puff pastry
single cream

Set oven at gas 6/450°F/220°C/Aga roasting oven.

Spread the marmalade over the base of a shallow round pie dish. Cut the oranges into thin slices (discard any pips), and arrange, overlapping, over the marmalade. Lightly oil the rim of the dish and cover with pastry pressing down on the oiled rim. Trim off all surplus pastry and prick the top lightly with a fork. Stand the dish on a baking tray and bake for 20-30mins. or until the pastry has risen and is browning. Remove from oven and allow to cool slightly before turning on to a hot, deep, serving dish. Serve hot or warm with single cream.

Lazy Cook tips - it is important to remember to take care when turning the pudding on to the serving plate because the marmalade is hot and runny. Oranges are at their best in winter and this is an excellent way of serving them.

Lemon Dream

I cannot take credit for this next recipe, it was passed on to me by a friend. We spent many happy family holidays with Barbara and Maurice on their lovely farm near Tavistock. Shortly after one visit she sent me a letter which included this recipe which we had all so much enjoyed. In the letter, which I still have, she talks of a trip to Plymouth to buy baby clothes, the expected baby is now a young man of 30 years.

serves 4
50gms (2ozs) butter – softened
25gms (1oz) plain flour
50gms (2ozs) caster sugar
2 large eggs – separated
1 lemon – juice and rind
150ml (¼pt) milk

Set oven at gas 3/300°F/150°C/Aga simering oven.

Put all ingredients, except the egg whites, into a processor and process together. Whisk the whites until they are stiff, add the processed ingredients and stir together. Pour into a pie or soufflé dish standing it in a meat tin and pour warm water to come half way up the dish. (see Bain Marie). Bake in the pre-set oven for 35-45mins. or until set.

Lazy Cook tips – the mixture might appear curdled before the whites are added but this does not matter. This pudding can be baked in one large dish or individual ramekins. A little extra sugar may be added if you prefer a sweeter taste. A lovely pudding to serve, light in texture with a sauce beneath.

Marmalade Crêpe with a Lemon Sauce and Single Cream

allow 2 crêpe per person (recipe on page 98)
orange marmalade
lemon curd
juice from a fresh lemon
thick single cream

Set oven at gas 6/450°F/220°C/Aga roasting oven.
Put a dessertspoon of marmalade on each crêpe and fold over to make a crescent shape. Place on a lightly oiled baking tray and heat in the pre-set oven (5-10mins). To make the sauce, put some lemon curd into a small pan with enough lemon juice to give it a good tangy flavour and stir it over a gentle heat until it is smooth and runny. To serve, place 2 filled crêpe in the centre of a dessert plate, slightly overlapping at one end, and pour lemon sauce down one side and cream down the other.

Lazy Cook tips – the filled crêpe can also be heated under a medium hot grill or in a microwave.

Recommended Menus

Burns Night Supper

For many years now we have celebrated Burns night with friends in the village   We take it in turns providing the supper or the whisky to accompany it and it's always a very jolly evening!

	page
Haggis	
Neeps	131
Gravy	29

∘ ∘ O ∘ ∘

Hot Orange Pudding and Cream   100

∘ ∘ O ∘ ∘

Cheese and Biscuits

∘ ∘ O ∘ ∘

Coffee

Valentine's Night Dinner

Burnt Red Pepper Soup   82
Bread rolls

o o O o o

Veal and Bacon Parcels with a Sundried Tomato Sauce   95
Pasta
Cauliflower Cheese Slices   127

o o O o o

Brandysnap Cups filled with Banana Slices, Spiced   99
Cream and Bitter Chocolate Lace

o o O o o

Cheese and Biscuits

o o O o o

Coffee

o o O o o

Peppermint Hearts   117

Mothering Sunday
a day when Dad and the family might choose to spoil Mother

Lunch

Tea

Easter

Easter is a very special event in the Christian calendar and a time for celebration. For many years we have invited friends to coffee and hot cross buns on Good Friday and on Easter Day we are often joined by more of the family for a special lunch and tea.

Easter Day Lunch page

Crown of Lamb with a Red Wine and Pesto Sauce   89
Minted New Potatoes
Spring Cabbage   129

o o O o o

Coffee Cracknell Meringue Ring   100

o o O o o

Cheese and Biscuits

o o O o o

Coffee

o o O o o

Mini Easter Eggs (ready made)

Tea

Easter Biscuits   109
Easter Bonnets   110

Index - Additional Recipes

Biscuits

Easter Biscuits

makes approx 24
100gms (4ozs) unsalted butter – softened
225gms (8ozs) plain flour
75gms (3ozs) caster sugar
a few good pinches cinnamon powder
grated rind of 1 lemon
1 small egg
good dash of brandy (about 1 tbls)
handful of currants for decoration

Set oven at gas 4/400°F/200°C/Aga baking oven.
Put the flour, sugar and cinnamon powder into a food processor and process for a few seconds.   Add all remaining ingredients, except the currants, and process until a ball of paste forms.   Roll to 2mm/¼" thickness and cut into rounds using a 7cm (3") fluted cutter.   Place on lightly oiled baking trays and press 3 currants into each.   Bake for 15-20mins.   Cool on a wire tray and store in an airtight container.

Lazy Cook tips – the amount of cooking time depends on how many biscuits are baked at a time, they should remain pale in colour when baked.   The three currants represent the Trinity – Father, Son and Holy Spirit.   They are a nice confection to serve at Easter.   Make in advance, they store well.

Easter Bonnets

1 pkt. round Rich Tea biscuits
1 pkt. marshmallows
a little royal icing of a coating consistency (recipe on page 118)
food colourings
sprays of flowers and other decorations from cake decorating shops

Put the biscuits, spaced well apart, on a wire tray and place a marshmallow in the centre of each.   Cover with royal icing and when set remove from the tray and decorate with flowers or other cake decorations.

Lazy Cook tips – colour the icing to make hats of a variety of colours.   If you are able to pipe, decorate some hats with squiggles of coloured icing. Alternatively they can be covered with ready-made fondant icing (available from cake decorating shops and supermarkets).   Roll out thinly before covering the biscuits.   This fondant can also be coloured, refer to instructions on packet.   A lovely confection to serve at Easter especially if catering for children who might also enjoy making them.

Gingerbread Biscuits and Shapes

100gms (4ozs) margarine – soften
225gms (8ozs) self-raising flour
100gms (4ozs) demerera sugar
1 teas. ground ginger
1 desst. black treacle
1 desst. golden syrup
1 desst. marmalade

Set oven at gas 4/400°F/200°C/Aga baking oven.
Put the flour, sugar and ginger into a food processor and process together for a few seconds.   Add all remaining ingredients and process into a ball of paste.   Roll on a lightly floured board or table to 2mm (¼") thickness and cut into shapes.   Place on a baking tray lightly oiled or covered with bake-o-glide, and bake for 15-20mins. or until set.   Remove from oven and cool on a wire tray.   Store in airtight tins.

Lazy Cook tips – cut into shapes to fit the occasion, i.e. for a bonfire or children's party cut into gingerbread men. For Christmas cut into stars and before baking pierce with a skewer to make a hole through which ribbon can be threaded and they can hang on a tree. Otherwise, make into ginger biscuits by putting small amounts of mixture on to a baking tray and flatten with a damp fork before baking.

Breadcrumbs *– fresh or dried*

Put pieces of bread (brown or white) into a food processor or liquidiser and process until crumbed. Use immediately or dry them on a tin tray in a cool oven or on top of an Aga. Store in airtight jars, they will keep for months.

Lazy Cook tips – a most useful ingredient to have in store. Use for coating ingredients before cooking, for topping savoury and sweet dishes, or for thickening soups.

Cakes

Chocolate Cake

serves 8-10
175gms (6ozs) butter – softened
125gms (5ozs) self-raising flour
100gms (4ozs) caster sugar
75gms (3ozs) drinking chocolate
3 large eggs
1 teas. vanilla essence
2 tbls. hot water
100gms (4ozs) bitter chocolate

Set oven at gas 4/400°F/200°C/Aga baking oven.
Line the base of a 20cm (8") round cake tin with bake-o-glide, or greaseproof, lightly oiled. Put the flour, sugar and drinking chocolate into a food processor and process for a few seconds. Add the butter, eggs, vanilla and boiling water and process for a few seconds until smooth Pour the mixture into the prepared tin and bake for 35-45mins. or until set. Remove from oven and turn on to a wire tray. Peel off the lining paper and grate chocolate over the surface of the cake while it is still hot. Serve when cold or store in an airtight tin.

Lazy Cook tips – this makes a very moist chocolate cake. The grated chocolate will set as the cake cools leaving a chocolate topping. For the richer cake split the cake when it is cold and sandwich it together with redcurrant jelly.

Christmas Cake

1 rich fruit cake (recipe on page 114)
brandy
lemon curd
almond paste (recipe on page 116)
cake board - 5cms (2") larger than the cake
royal icing with a few spots glycerine added (recipe on page 118)
Christmas cake decorations
cake band and ribbon

Prick the top of the cake with a metal skewer and add brandy poured from a tablespoon and leave for a few minutes to soak in.   Spread the top with a little lemon curd and cover with almond paste.   Stand the cake on the board securing it with a little lemon curd.   Tie a band of greaseproof round to protrude approx. 2cms (1") above the cake and pour in royal icing to cover the almond paste.   Leave to set overnight or for a few days. Remove the band of greaseproof easing it off with a palette knife and decorate the top as you wish   Tie with a cake band and ribbon.

Lazy Cook tips – readymade almond paste, or marzipan, and fondant icing can be used, these are available from specialist cake decorating shops or supermarkets.   Once the cake has been cut store it in an airtight tin.

Ginger Cake

50gms (2ozs) margarine – soften
50gms (2ozs) lard – soften
175gms (6ozs) self-raising flour
75gms (3ozs) soft cane sugar
½ teas. ground ginger
1 teas. fresh lemon juice
3 large eggs
50gms (2ozs) ginger preserved in syrup – cut up
1 tbls ginger syrup

Set oven at gas 4/400°F/200°C/Aga baking oven.
Lightly oil a 450gm (1 lb) loaf tin.   Put all the dry ingredients into a food
processor and process together for a few seconds.   Add all remaining
ingredients and process until smooth.   Pour into the prepared tin and bake
in the pre-set oven for 30-40mins. or until set.   Turn on to a wire tray to
cool   Store in an airtight tin.

Rich Fruit Cake for Christmas and Special Occasions

to fit a 25cm (10") round tin
275gms (10ozs) butter - softened
225gms (8ozs) dark cane or muscavado sugar
1 tbls. molasses
6 large eggs
400gms (14ozs) plain flour
1 teas. mixed spice
450gms (1 lb) currants
275gms (10ozs) sultanas
275gms (10ozs) raisins
175gms (6ozs) mixed chopped peel
100gms (4ozs) glacé cherries – leave whole
100gms (4ozs) flaked almonds – browned and crushed in hand
brandy – to be added after baking

Set oven at gas 3/300°F/150°C/Aga simmering oven.
Line the base and sides of the cake tin with greaseproof (no need to
grease).   Cream the butter and sugar together, add the eggs, molasses,
flour and spice and mix to a smooth soft consistency.   Mix all the
remaining ingredients together (except the brandy) and stir into the butter
mixture.   Pack into the prepared tin and level the top.   Stand the tin on a
baking tray and bake in the pre-set oven for 6-8hrs or until set.   Test by
putting a metal skewer into the centre, if it comes out clean the cake is
baked.   Remove from oven and allow to cool a little before turning on to a
wire tray.   Prick all over the top with a metal skewer and pour a liberal
amount of brandy into the cake.   Wrap in greaseproof and foil and store in
a cool dry place until required for decoration.

Lazy Cook tips – oven temperatures vary so much and I recommend you look at the cake after 4hrs. A second indication of the cake being baked is when cracks appear round the edge. I was given this recipe many years ago by an Aunt and I use it for all Christmas, wedding or special occasion cakes, it is rich and moist. Pour more brandy into the cake before decorating. If possible bake two or three months before serving, it will improve on keeping.

Simnel Cake

1 rich fruit cake (recipe on page 114)
almond paste (recipe on page 116)
apricot jam – melted
2 egg shell halves
1 fluffy chicken – buy from a cake decorating shop!
cake band
cake board or plate

Follow the recipe for rich fruit cake but put half the mixture in the tin then cover with a layer of almond paste before topping with the remaining mixture. Bake as for the rich fruit cake. To decorate, spread apricot jam over the top of the cake then cover with almond paste. Mark a circle in the centre (approx. 10cms/4") and cover this with small balls of almond paste, sticking them into place with a little jam. Mark the outside edge by pressing a fork into the almond paste. Stand the cake on a baking tray and place under a grill to lightly brown the almond paste. Allow to cool before placing two halves of egg shell in the centre of the circle and place the chicken inside. Fix a cake band round the cake and place on a board or serving dish.

Lazy cook tips – mark the centre circle using a pastry cutter or an upturned glass. If you cook by Aga and have no grill, brown the top by putting the cake at the top of the roasting oven for a few minutes. Alternatively brown using a chef's blowlamp (follow the manufacturer's instructions before use).

Chocolates and Icings

Almond Chocolates

almond paste (recipe below)
bitter chocolate – melted
whole almonds – with skins

Mould almond paste into a sausage shape and cut into pieces approx. 10mm (½") thick.   Place on foil and leave for a few hours to dry before dropping into melted chocolate to coat all over.   Put back on to foil, press a whole almond into the top and when the chocolate has set hard store in a box.

Almond Paste

350gms (12ozs) ground almonds
275gms (10ozs) caster sugar
275gms (10ozs) icing sugar
4 tbls. brandy
2 tbls. fresh lemon juice
1 teas. orange flower water
a few spots almond essence
1 medium sized egg
1 yolk

Mix the almonds and sugars together in a large bowl and make a well in the centre.   Whisk all remaining ingredients together, pour into the well and work together to form a paste.   Shape or roll on a surface sifted with icing sugar.

Lazy Cook tips – try not to over-knead this paste, it will extract the oil from the almonds and will eventually cause a top icing to discolour.   Use as soon as it is made, storage will cause it to become crisp on the surface and difficult to handle.   If it is too sticky, add a little more sifted icing sugar; if too dry add a little more brandy or lemon juice.   This quantity is sufficient to cover a 24cm (10") round or square cake.

Chocolate Tablets

Melt bitter, milk or white chocolate and drop from a teaspoon on to foil and spread into a disc shape. Cover either with, browned flaked almonds, walnut halves, crystalised ginger pieces or a mixture of raisins and nuts. When the chocolate has hardened store in a box. Peel from the foil to serve.

Holly Leaves and Berries

For the leaves – colour a small amount of ready made fondant icing with green food colouring. Roll thinly using a little sifted icing sugar to prevent sticking. Cut into small, medium or large holly leaves using appropriate cutters (available from specialist cake decoration shops). Bend each leaf slightly before placing on an empty egg box to dry. Store in a box.

For the berries – colour a very small amount of ready made fondant icing with red food colouring and work between index finger and thumb into a berry. When dry store in a box.

Peppermint Hearts

450gms (1 lb) icing sugar
1 egg white
1 tbls. water
1 teas. peppermint essence (or a few spots peppermint oil)
green food colouring

Put the icing sugar into a food processor and process for a few seconds. Lightly whisk the egg white with a tablespoon of cold water, a spot of green food colouring and the peppermint essence. Pour through the funnel with the machine switched on, until it forms a ball. Remove from the processor and work to a pliable paste with sieved icing sugar. Roll to 5mm (¼") thickness and cut with a heart shaped cutter. Place on foil lightly sifted with icing sugar and leave to dry. Store in a box.

Lazy Cook tips – avoid adding too much colouring by dropping it from a metal skewer. For ease of rolling, take small quantities from the processor at a time. Cover the remainder with a damp cloth or kitchen paper. The dried creams can be decorated either with melted bitter chocolate trailed from a spoon, or completely dipped in melted bitter chocolate. Leave on the foil until dry. Store in a box.

Royal Icing

450gms (1 lb) icing sugar
2 egg whites – lightly whisk with a fork
a spot of blue food colouring

Put the icing sugar into a food processor and process for a few seconds before adding the egg whites, switch off when the consistency is smooth. Add a spot of blue food colouring and adjust to the consistency required by adding a little more icing sugar if it is too runny, a little warm water if is too stiff.

Lazy Cook tips – avoid adding too much colouring by dropping it from a metal skewer. Once the consistency is decided the icing can be coloured by adding food colourings (available from specialist cake decoration shops). The blue colouring listed in the ingredients merely makes the white whiter, add more to colour it blue. Always keep the icing covered with a damp cloth or damp kitchen roll to prevent a skin forming. It will store for 2-3 days when covered, keep the cloth damp and store in a cold room. Useful for decorating Christmas or special occasion cakes when a few spots of glycerine should be added to prevent the icing becoming rock hard. I recommend a half teaspoon glycerine per 450gms (1 lb) made icing.

Mayonnaise

1 large egg
1 desst. cider or wine vinegar
½ teas. sugar
½ teas. mustard powder
½ teas. ground white pepper
½ teas. salt
300ml (½pt) sunflower oil

Put all the ingredients except the oil into a food processor or liquidiser and process for a few seconds then, with the machine still running, gradually add the oil until the mayonnaise thickens to the required consistency. Put into a jar with a lid and store in a fridge.

Lazy Cook tips – a mixture of oils can be used to vary the flavour. If the mayonnaise is too thick thin it down by stirring in a little warm water, or fruit juice. It is a very useful ingredient to have in store especially at party time.

Meringues

To make
To each egg white allow 50gms (2ozs) caster sugar. Whip the whites until they are stiff and dry (I describe this as a cottonwool texture), before stirring in the sugar. The meringue is then ready to be shaped on to baking trays covered with household parchment or bake-o-glide. When shaped, put into a low oven to dry (gas 2/200°F/100°C/Aga simmering oven (the latter with the door slightly ajar). They are dry when they will peel from the baking paper. Allow a few minutes for the meringue shapes to become cold before storing in airtight containers, or polythene bags.

Lazy Cook tips – if a bubbling of liquid appears, this is because the sugar has not been completely folded into the egg whites. This will add a slightly toffee texture to the meringue. Cream, which is the most popular ingredient to serve with meringues, will soften the texture and make for ease of slicing.

Meringue Shapes

A store of meringue shapes is always useful and they keep for months in airtight containers or polythene bags.

Meringue Bases and Plates

Spread the meringue into rounds in sizes from 5cms (2") to 25cms (10") in diameter.

Meringue Baskets

Make in various sizes from 5cms (2") to 25cms (10") in diameter. Spread bases with an outer rim of meringue (dropped from a spoon), to form a centre cavity. Make in round or rectangular shapes.

Meringue Rings

Spread meringue into rings in sizes from 7cms (3") to 25cms (10") leaving a centre cavity.

Petites Meringues

Drop meringue from a teaspoon on to a prepared baking tray. Serve by dipping in melted chocolate or sandwiching with whipped cream.

Preserves

Apple Purée

Peel, core and slice bramley apples into a pan with just enough water to moisten the base. Add several whole cloves (optional), place lid on pan and cook over a gentle heat until the apples pulp and rise in the pan. Remove from the heat and use immediately or allow to become cold and store, covered, in a fridge or cold larder. Use within 4 days. To freeze, remove the cloves and pack the cold purée into freezer bags of varying sizes.

Apple Purée made from Frozen Apple Slices

Peel, core and slice bramley apples and pack into freezer bags and freeze. To purée, remove the slices from the freezer bag and put into a pan with the base moistened with cold water. Add several whole cloves (optional), put lid on pan and cook over a gentle heat until pulped. Use immediately or store as mentioned in the above recipe.

Lazy Cook tips – apple purée is a most useful ingredient to have in store. Serve as a sauce or add to soups, sauces, casseroles and many sweet dishes. Sweeten to taste but if good bramleys are used they will need little or no sweetening.

Mincemeat

makes approx 7 x 350gms (¾lb) jars
450gms (1 lb) raisins
225gms (8ozs) sultanas
350gms (12ozs) currants
225gms (8ozs) mixed peel
100gms (4ozs) flaked almonds
225gms (8ozs) shredded suet
175gms (6ozs) dark brown sugar
2 large cooking apples – peel, core and chop
2 lemons – juice and zest
½ teas. cinnamon powder
½ teas. mixed spice
225ml (8 fl.ozs) brandy

Put the raisins, sultanas, currants, almonds and apple into a food processor and process for a few seconds to mince. Transfer to a large mixing bowl and stir in the remaining ingredients. Pack into clean, dry jars, cover with a disc of greaseproof and a lid. Label and store in a cold, dry place for several months before using.

Lazy Cook tips – home-made mincemeat is much less sweet than a bought variety. It needs to be made in advance so that the flavours have time to blend. I have often made it as early as January using up any fruit left over from Christmas. A pot of home-made mincemeat makes a very acceptable small Christmas present.

Orange Marmalade

makes approx 10 x 350gms (¾ lb) jars
900gms (2lbs) Seville oranges
1 lemon
1¾ ltr (3pts) water
1¾ kg (4 lbs) granulated sugar

Scrub the oranges and lemons. Cut each into quarters, cut the flesh away (including pips) and put into a piece of muslin and tie. Put the peel into a food processor and process until chopped. Put into a preserving, (or a very large pan) with the muslin bag and water. Boil for 15mins. without lid. Remove from heat and leave for 3-4hrs. or overnight. Bring back to boiling point and boil for 10mins. without lid. Remove from heat, remove the muslin bag and stir in the sugar until it has completely dissolved. Return to heat and boil rapidly for 15mins. Remove from heat and put a little on a plate. Put in fridge and when cold push a finger through the centre, if a skin forms and the channel formed does not close, the marmalade is ready for potting. Remove any scum which will have collected on the top and stir before pouring into hot, clean jars. Cover with a disc of greaseproof and a lid. When cold label and store in a cold dry place.

Lazy Cook tips – I find marmalade making very therapeutic and for this reason if no other, I spend a little time slicing the peel with a sharp knife rather than processing it. A preserving pan is best in which to make boiled preserves, otherwise a very large saucepan should be used because when the ingredients boil rapidly they also rise in the pan. Do not allow them to boil over, reduce the heat if necessary. The sugar must completely dissolve before the ingredients are reboiled, I stir it in for 5mins. then test by poking the base of the pan and any undissolved crystals will be felt. If the marmalade is not set on the first testing, reboil and test every 2mins. If you cook by Aga, after the initial boiling, put the pan in the simmering oven for a few hours to soften the skins then continue as in the recipe. A popular preserve to have in store to serve on toast or in many recipes.

Rice
to boil (brown or white)

For most recipes I use short grain brown rice purchased from a Health Food shop. I boil and store it as follows –

Allow 50gms (2ozs) rice per person. Put the grains into a wire sieve and rinse under a cold running tap until the water runs clear. Scatter the washed grains into a large pan containing lots of boiling water, stir well, bring to a simmer, cover and simmer gently for 15-20mins. or until cooked but of a nutty texture. Strain the cooked rice into a sieve and rinse well under a running cold water tap until the water runs clear before serving. The cooked grains should remain whole, tender and separate. If the rice is to be served hot, rinse after cooking in boiling water poured from a kettle. Boiled rice can be stored in a covered container in a fridge. Serve cold from the fridge or reheat by rinsing in boiling water, or in a microwave. Boiled rice is a most useful ingredient to have in store.

Rice with Sweetcorn and Herbs

serves 4-6
225gms (8ozs) boiled rice (recipe on page 123)
1 x 400gm. tin sweetcorn in water
4 pickled cucumbers – slice
1 teas. mixed dried herbs
freshly ground pepper

To serve hot – empty the sweetcorn, including the water, into a large saucepan and bring to a simmer.   Add the cooked rice, cucumbers and herbs and stir over a gentle heat until hot.   Strain off any excess liquid before serving.

To serve cold – drain the liquid from the sweetcorn before mixing all ingredients together.

Savoury Rice

Stir cooked peas, sweetcorn and mixed herbs into cooked rice.   Add a few good pinches of curry powder and a little single cream and stir well before serving, hot or cold.

Wild Rice

This is not a rice but a grain, mostly grown in North America.   It adds an interesting contrast of colour and texture when mixed with brown or white rice but does not contain the nutritional value of either of these. Prepare as instructed by the manufacture.

Stock Making the Lazy Cook Way

There is something very wholesome and satisfying about adding a little jellied stock to a recipe. My method of making stock, though not traditional, gives good quick results and a stock superior to any which can be bought.

Fish – put uncooked fish bones, skin and heads into a pan and cover with cold water. Bring slowly to boil, without lid, skim the top then add 8-10 peppercorns and a bayleaf. Place lid on pan and simmer for 20mins. Remove from heat and strain into a basin. Follow instructions for storing or freezing as for meat stock.

Ham – strain the liquid from a cooked ham or bacon joint, (recipe on page 59). Follow directions for storing as for meat stock.

Meat – put bones/carcass, cooked or uncooked into a pan. Cover with cold water, bring slowly to boil, without lid. Skim the top, place lid on pan and simmer for 2-4 hrs (if you cook by Aga this should be done in the simmering oven). Strain into a basin and when cold store in a fridge and use within 2 days, removing the fat which will have set on the surface. Alternatively freeze by removing the surface fat and pack the stock into freezer bags. For convenience of use I freeze stock in bags of varying sizes.

Vegetable – strain all liquid from cooked vegetables into a jug and when cold cover and store in a fridge. Use within 2 days.

Vegetables

Red Cabbage - baked

1 red cabbage
1 tbls. demerera sugar
2 tbls. cider vinegar
4 tbls. water

Set oven at gas 6/450°F/220°C/Aga roasting oven.
Slice the cabbage and put into an ovenproof casserole. Add the remaining ingredients, put lid on the casserole and put into the pre-set oven for 10mins. before reducing the temperature to gas 3/300°F/150°C/Aga simmering oven. Continue to bake for one hour. Serve straight from the oven or allow to become cold then store in a fridge or cold larder. Reheat in a pan over a gentle heat, or in the oven.

Lazy Cook tips – I find red cabbage a most useful winter vegetable, it has a good colour and the flavour isn't lost when it is reheated.

Beetroot

to cook
Cut off the stalk to within 2cms (1") of the beetroot. Put the beetroots into a pan, cover with cold water and simmer, with lid on pan, for about an hour (depending on the size of the beetroots). Strain off the cooking liquid and discard. Peel and slice the beetroots before serving.

Lazy Cook tips – beetroots have a deliciously sweet flavour and I serve them in many ways. Once cooked they will store, in a fridge or cold larder for 2-3 days. If you cook by Aga the simmering process should be done in the simmering oven.

Bisley Beets

serves 4-6
4 large cooked beetroots (recipe on page 126)
1 large onion – skin and slice
2 tbls. cider vinegar
1 tbls. dememera sugar
1 teas. Dijon mustard
1 tbls. chutney

Set oven at gas 6/450°F/220°C/Aga roasting oven.
Soften the onion in a little boiling water with lid on pan.   Skin and slice the beetroots and layer into a shallow ovenproof dish.   Using a slotted spoon strain the onion rings from the liquid and put over the beetroot slices.   To the onion liquid add all the remaining ingredients and simmer together before pouring over the onion rings.   Cover with foil and put into the pre-set oven (or a microwave), until it is hot throughout.

Lazy Cook tips – this recipe can be prepared a day or two in advance of serving, store, covered, in a fridge or cold larder.   Serve as a light meal with hot bread, or as a vegetable course with meat or fish.

Cauliflower Cheese Slices

to make 4-6
1 medium sized cauliflower
225gms (8ozs) Stilton cheese

Trim the stalk and outer leaves of the cauliflower and cut into slices approx. 1cm (½") thick.   Boil in a little water until they begin to soften, remove from pan and put into a shallow ovenproof dish, or baking tin, spaced a little apart.   Cover each slice with thin slices of Stilton and put under a hot grill or in a hot oven (gas 6/450°F/220°C/Aga roasting oven) until the cheese has melted.   Using a fish slice, remove on to individual plates to serve.

Lazy Cook tips – if the slices should break up during boiling, reshape them before adding the cheese. This recipes demonstrates an attractive way of serving this most versatile of vegetables. When the cheese has melted the shape of the cauliflower is apparent, dotted with cheese, they look so pretty and the flavours are excellent. Much lower in calories than cauliflower cheese, and quicker to make.

Celery Hearts with Fresh Lemon and Sage

serves 4
2 celery hearts
1 lemon – juice and grated zest
fresh or dried sage leaves

Cut the celery hearts into 6-8 lengths and boil in a little water, with lid on pan, until they begin to soften. Strain off the cooking liquid. Put the hearts into a serving dish, pour over a good squeeze of lemon juice and scatter with sage and grated lemon zest.

Lazy Cook tips – celery hearts are expensive, it is more economical to buy a head and use the top for winter salads or adding to soups and casseroles.

Buttered Sprouts

Remove any damaged outer leaves, wash the sprouts and cut an "x" into the base of each. Boil in a little water, with lid on pan, until they are cooked to your liking. Strain off the cooking liquid, add a nut of butter to the pan and when melted add the sprouts and stir over a gentle heat until the sprouts are glazed in butter. Serve hot.

Curly Cabbage with Fresh Orange

1 curly cabbage
1 fresh orange – juice and zest

Remove any outer damaged leaves then slice and wash the cabbage. Cook in a little boiling water with lid on pan, until tender. Strain off the cooking liquid. Add the juice and zest of one orange to the pan, add the cabbage and stir over a gentle heat until the orange juice has been absorbed. Serve.

Spring Cabbage

1 cabbage
a nut of butter
freshly grated nutmeg

Remove any outer damaged leaves and discard. Trim the base of the stalk and break off the large outer cabbage leaves, cut out the stalk, slice the leaves. Cut the centre heart into quarters and cut out the stalk before slicing. Wash the cabbage and cook in a little boiling water for 2-3mins. or until cooked to your liking, with lid on pan. Strain off the water, add a nut of butter to the pan and when melted add the cabbage, season with freshly grated nutmeg and stir over a gentle heat until the cabbage is glazed in butter. Serve hot.

Curried Vegetables

a selection of left over vegetables
single cream
curry powder – mild, medium or hot

Put all ingredients into a pan and stir over a gentle heat until hot. Serve hot or cold.

Macedoine of Vegetables

Roughly equal quantities of the following –
carrot – cut into small cubes
celery – cut into small cubes
frozen peas
frozen sweetcorn
nut of butter
sprinkling of fresh parsley if available.

Put all the vegetables into a pan, cover with cold water, bring to a boil and boil for 2mins. Strain off the cooking liquid. Add a nut of butter and the parsley to the vegetables and stir before serving.

Lazy Cook tips – this recipe can be served as a vegetable course or added to cooked rice or pasta, or, when cold, stirred into mayonnaise. Whichever you choose it will present a colourful and tasty dish.

Mixed Vegetables

carrots – cut into julienne strips
calabrese – break into small florets
baby corn
nut of butter

Boil all the vegetables together in a little water until cooked to your liking Strain off the cooking liquid, put the vegetables into a hot dish and smear with a little butter before serving.

Potatoes Baked in their Jackets

Set oven at gas 6/450°F/220°C/Aga roasting oven. Scrub the poatoes, mark each with an "x" and bake in the pre-set oven for an hour or until crisp. Serve hot with butter or a savoury filling of your choice.

Potato Gratinée

serves 4-6
900gms (2 lbs) potatoes
garlic – optional
50gms (2ozs) butter – melted
nutmeg – freshly grated

Set oven at gas 6/450°F/220°C/Aga roasting oven.
Lightly oil a shallow ovenproof dish.   Peel the potatoes, slice very thinly
and layer with the garlic into the prepared dish.   Pour melted butter over
the top and season with freshly grated nutmeg.   Bake in the pre-set oven
for 30mins to 1 hr. depending on the quantity being baked.   Serve hot
from the oven.

*Lazy Cook tips – this is a recipe which has to be prepared and baked
immediately otherwise the potatoes will turn black.   A delicious way to
serve potatoes in winter.*

Swede with Fresh Lemon Juice

Peel a swede and cut into small pieces.   Add to a pan of boiling water and
boil, with lid on pan, until soft.   Strain off the cooking liquid and mash the
swede.   Stir in the juice of half a lemon and season with freshly ground
pepper.   Serve hot.

Salads

Winter Salads

Although lettuce, tomatoes, cucumbers and many other salad ingredients are now available all the year round, I still prefer to reserve these for summer enjoyment. I sometimes use a few prepared salad leaves to garnish certain recipes, but during the autumn and winter months I prefer to keep my salad ingredients to those given below.

A Daily Salad for Healthy Autumn and Winter Months

per person –
1 small carrot
a few pieces of celery
1 spring onion

Wash all ingredients before cutting into pieces of a similar size before serving. I recommend these salad ingredients are eaten each day as part of a healthy winter diet. They can be put into a polythene bag and included in a packed lunch box, or added to a winter picnic.

Watercress Sandwiches

Spread a little creamed cheese on to slices of wholemeal or white bread and sandwich together with lots of watercress and a little freshly ground salt – simply delicious.

Cookery Terms and Abbreviations
(a Lazy Cook's shorthand)

Au gratin - a topping of cheese and breadcrumbs, usually over a sauce or cooked vegetables

Blanche – to cook in boiling water for a short time
               to whiten

Bain-marie – a water bath in which certain foods are baked inside or on top of the oven to prevent them drying or cooking too quickly.   Also useful for keeping certain sauces hot before serving.

b/b – bread and butter

b/c's – breadcrumbs

Boil – lots of bubbles
      par boil – to put ingredients into cold water and bring to a boil
      rapid boil – lots of bubbles rising in the pan

Bouchée – small cases made from puff pastry served with savoury or sweet fillings, cold or hot

Celery – a head – the whole celery
      a stick – a piece from the celery head

Chine – to remove the bone from a joint of meat, usually best end or loin of lamb, so that individual chops can be cut.

Degorger – to extract strong flavours

Desst. – dessertspoon

f.g.p. – freshly ground pepper

Fillet – to remove all bones

Flavour – to extract flavour – cut ingredients small and cook slowly as in soup, chutney and jam making.

to seal in flavour – to brown ingredients quickly in hot fat

g/a's – ground almonds

Gratinée – a topping of breadcrumbs

Green – unsmoked, usually refers to ham or bacon

Knead – when handling bread dough

Knead Lightly – when handling pastry or scone dough

Marinade – to leave in soak, often in a brine of wine, oil and herbs

p.f. – plain flour

Pate – a pastry or dough

Paté – a savoury paste

Press – to stand a weight on cooked or prepared good

Purée– ingredients made smooth by liquidising, processing or passing through a sieve

Roulade – to roll

Roux – a paste made from butter and flour as a base for a sauce

s & p – salt and pepper

Sauté – to cook quickly in hot fat

Seasoned flour - plain flour with either salt, pepper, herbs or other ingredients added. Used for coating ingredients before they are cooked to prevent sticking or to introduce additional flavours

s/d toms – sun-dried tomatoes

s.r. – self-raising flour

Simmer – gentle bubbles
        gently simmer – occasional bubbles

Sweat – to soften vegetables in butter with lid on pan

tbls. - tablespoon

teas. – teaspoon

t.o.m. – top of milk

Hob Temperatures

Gentle simmer – an occasional bubble
Simmer – a more regular bubble
Boil – constant bubbles
Rapid boil – constant bubbles rising in pan

Aga owners should start the simmering process on the hobs then transfer the pan to the simmering oven.

Oven Temperatures

These can vary considerably and the temperatures given below, and the ones quoted in the recipes in this book, should be used as guidelines and adjusted according to your cooker.

	Gas	F	C	Aga
Warm	1–2	25°-250°	10°-120°	bottom left (4-oven)
Moderate/ Simmering	3-4	250°-350°	120°-160°	top left (4-oven)
Baking	4-5	375°-400°	180°-200°	bottom (2-oven) bottom R (4-oven)
Roasting	6-7	450°-500°	220°-250°	top (2-oven) top R (4-oven)

2-oven Aga owners can reduce the oven temperature by using the large baking sheet, a cake-baker, or bain-marie (please refer to booklet supplied by Aga).

Recommended Equipment

A food processor is as essential for Lazy Cooking as is a passport for travel abroad. In addition, a good chopping board and several sharp knives, a selection of pots and pans and casseroles of the best quality you can afford. Other standard equipment should include baking trays, cooling trays, a grater, various spoons and ladles. A measuring jug, wooden spoons and spatulas.

Purchase a variety of colourful serving dishes and plates and, if you are fortunate enough to have inherited them, take Granny's lovely old plates and dishes out of the cupboard and use them to show off your meals. First impressions are important and good presentation is one of the secrets of success whether you are serving a savoy cabbage or a whole wild salmon. Presentation does not have to be elaborate, often the simplest is the most eye-catching. Always avoid overcrowding ingredients on to too small a dish and remember, too many flavours served at any one meal will confuse the palate – keep it simple and it will be good.

Recommended Store Cupboard

The choice of store cupboard is a personal one.   In addition to basic cupboard, fridge and freezer supplies, I recommend the following "key" ingredients which for me, are essential for Lazy Cooking.

Anchovies - fresh, preserved in oil
Bacon
   back
   lardons
   streaky
Bags of frozen stock
Blackcurrants – jars (in syrup)
Cheeses
   cheddar
   Parmesan
   stilton
Chocolat Charbonnel (ready grated chocolate)
Chutney
Cider vinegar
Cocktail blinis
Dried breadcrumbs
Dried chestnuts
Dried fruit
   apricots
   bags of fruit salad
   raisins
   prunes
Mushroom ketchup
Mustards
   Dijon
   English (powder)
   grain
Horseradish cream
Marmalade
Orange flower water

Orange juice (Britvic 150ml cans)
Packets of home-made crêpe
Pastry cases (ready baked)
Pesto
Piccalilli
Pitta bread
Pitted black olives
Sardines in oil
Smoked salmon
Soups
   condensed – chicken, mushroom
   lobster bisque
Sundried tomatoes (jars, in oil)
Sundried tomato purée – tubes (keep in fridge once opened)
Tomatoes – tins, all sizes
Trifle sponges
Wines and Spirits
   brandy
   ginger wine
   wine – red, white

Weights and Measures

as used in recipes in this book

Dry measurements

25gms	=	1 oz
50gms	=	2 ozs
100gms	=	4 ozs
175gms	=	6 ozs
225gms	=	8 ozs
700gms	=	1½ lbs
900gms	=	2 lbs
1 kg	=	2 lbs 4 ozs
1¾ kg	=	4 lbs

Liquid measurements

100ml	= 4 fl.ozs
150ml	= ¼ pint (1 gill)
300ml	= ½ pint
425ml	= ¾ pint
600ml	= 1 pint
1 litre	= 1¾ pints
1¾ ltrs	= 3 pints

Complete Index